Bond
No.1 for exam success

MW00358593

Verbal Reasoning

Assessment Papers

10–11+ years

Book 1

OXFORD
UNIVERSITY PRESS

OXFORD
UNIVERSITY PRESS

Great Clarendon Street, Oxford, OX2 6DP, United Kingdom

Oxford University Press is a department of the University of Oxford.
It furthers the University's objective of excellence in research,
scholarship, and education by publishing worldwide. Oxford is
a registered trade mark of Oxford University Press in the UK and in
certain other countries

Text © J M Bond and Frances Down 2020

The moral rights of the authors have been asserted

First published in 2015

This new edition 2020

British Library Cataloguing in Publication Data
Data available

978-0-19-277644-0

10 9 8 7 6 5 4 3 2 1

Paper used in the production of this book is a natural, recyclable
product made from wood grown in sustainable forests.
The manufacturing process conforms to the environmental
regulations of the country of origin.

Printed in China

Acknowledgements

The publishers would like to thank the following for permissions to
use copyright material:

Page make-up: OKS Prepress, India
Cover illustrations: Lo Cole

Although we have made every effort to trace and contact all
copyright holders before publication this has not been possible in all
cases. If notified, the publisher will rectify any errors or omissions at
the earliest opportunity.

The publisher would like to thank Michellejoy Hughes for assisting
with the compilation of the expanded answers.

Links to third party websites are provided by Oxford in good faith
and for information only. Oxford disclaims any responsibility for
the materials contained in any third party website referenced in
this work.

Before you get started

What is Bond?

This book is part of the Bond Assessment Papers series for verbal reasoning, which provides a **thorough and progressive course in verbal reasoning** from ages six to twelve. It builds up reasoning skills from book to book over the course of the series.

Bond's verbal reasoning resources are ideal preparation for the 11+ and other secondary school selection exams.

How does the scope of this book match real exam content?

Verbal Reasoning 10–11+ Book 1 and *Book 2* are the core Bond 11+ books. Each paper is **pitched at the level of a typical 11+ exam** and practises a wide range of questions drawn from the four distinct groups of verbal reasoning question types: sorting words, selecting words, anagrams, coded sequences and logic. The papers are fully in line with 11+ and other selective exams for this age group but are designed to practise a **wider variety of skills and question types** than most other practice papers so that children are always challenged to think – and don't get bored repeating the same question type again and again. We believe that variety is the key to effective learning. It helps children 'think on their feet' and cope with the unexpected: it is surprising how often children come out of verbal reasoning exams having met question types they have not seen before.

What does the book contain?

- **14 papers** – each one contains 80 questions.
- **Tutorial links throughout** – 📖 – this icon appears in the margin next to the questions. It indicates links to the relevant section in *How to do ...11+ Verbal Reasoning*, our invaluable subject guide that offers explanations and practice for all core question types.
- **Scoring devices** – there are score boxes in the margins and a Progress Chart on page 68. The chart is a visual and motivating way for children to see how they are doing. It also turns the score into a percentage that can help decide what to do next.
- **Next Steps Planner** – advice on what to do after finishing the papers can be found on the inside back cover.
- **Answers** – located in an easily-removed central pull-out section.

How can you use this book?

One of the great strengths of Bond Assessment Papers is their flexibility. They can be used at home, in school and by tutors to:

- **set timed formal practice tests** – allow about 45 minutes per paper in line with standard 11+ demands. Reduce the suggested time limit by five minutes to practise working at speed.

- provide **bite-sized chunks** for regular practice
- **highlight strengths and weaknesses** in the core skills
- identify **individual needs**
- set **homework**
- follow a **complete 11+ preparation strategy** alongside *The Parents' Guide to the 11+* (see below).

It is best to start at the beginning and work through the papers in order. If you are using the book as part of a careful run in to the 11+, we suggest that you also have two other essential Bond resources close at hand:

How to do ... 11+ Verbal Reasoning: the subject guide that explains all the question types practised in this book. Use the cross-reference icons to find the relevant sections.

The Parents' Guide to the 11+: the step-by-step guide to the whole 11+ experience. It clearly explains the 11+ process, provides guidance on how to assess children, helps you to set complete action plans for practice and explains how you can use the *Verbal Reasoning 10–11⁺ Book 1* and *Book 2* as part of a strategic run-in to the exam.

See the inside front cover for more details of these books.

What does a child's score mean and how can it be improved?

It is unfortunately impossible to guarantee that a child will pass the 11+ exam if they achieve a certain score on any practice book or paper. Success on the day depends on a host of factors, including the scores of the other children sitting the test. However, we can give some guidance on what a score indicates and how to improve it.

If children colour in the Progress Chart on page 68, this will give an idea of present performance in percentage terms. The Next Steps Planner inside the back cover will help you to decide what to do next to help a child progress. It is always valuable to go over wrong answers with children. If they are having trouble with any particular question type, follow the tutorial links to *How to do ... 11+ Verbal Reasoning* for step-by-step explanations and further practice.

Don't forget the website...!

Visit www.bond11plus.co.uk for lots of advice, information and suggestions on everything to do with Bond, the 11+ and helping children to do their best.

B 1

1–5 Look at these groups of words.

A	B	C	D	E
asthma	spotty	fig	celery	mole
flu	freckled	grape	swede	seal

Choose the correct group for each of the words below. Write in the letter.

clear ___   sprouts ___   fever ___   ewe ___   currant ___   bean ___

pony ___   tanned ___   damson ___   cough ___

5

Underline one word in the brackets which is most opposite in meaning to the word in capitals.

B 6

Example   WIDE   (broad   most   vague   long   <u>narrow</u>   motorway)

6 COOL   (warm   hot   cold   icy   frozen)

7 INACCURATE   (spontaneous   precise   casual   easy-going   forced)

8 SIMPLE   (idle   comfortable   easy   soft   complicated)

9 ASSIST   (hinder   help   aid   handle   halt)

10 INITIAL   (last   early   letter   name   first)

5

Underline the one word in the brackets which will go equally well with both the pairs of words outside the brackets.

B 5

Example   rush, attack   cost, fee   (price, hasten, strike, <u>charge</u>, money)

11 sugar, honey   dessert, pudding   (meal, cake, sweet, tea, coffee)

12 apartment, rooms   level, even   (house, bungalow, flat, smooth, straight)

13 speck, stain   see, notice   (vision, clean, bit, spot, catch)

14 pot, cup   attack, beat up   (hit, pail, break, pan, mug)

15 pennant, banner   tire, exhaust   (stone, flag, weary, wilt, sign)

5

Find the letter which will end the first word and start the second word.

B 10

Example   peac (<u>h</u>) ome

16 kin (___) esk   **17** fis (___) ool

18 lin (___) ind   **19** oxe (___) ail

20 bor (___) ast

5

Find the missing number by using the two numbers outside the brackets in the same way as the other sets of numbers.

Example   2 [8] 4   3 [18] 6   5 [25] 5

21 7 [12] 5   3 [11] 8   5 [__] 9

22 20 [5] 4   16 [4] 4   18 [__] 3

23 7 [13] 4   3 [7] 2   6 [__] 9

24 8 [12] 3   6 [18] 6   5 [__] 4

25 9 [5] 2   8 [1] 5   11 [__] 7

Underline two words, one from each group, that go together to form a new word. The word in the first group always comes first.

Example   (hand, <u>green</u>, for)   (light, <u>house</u>, sure)

26 (to, for, has)   (own, many, got)

27 (over, shut, open)   (in, take, torn)

28 (near, after, under)   (some, ground, before)

29 (point, aim, finger)   (side, bottom, print)

30 (am, is, be)   (his, low, high)

Find the four-letter word hidden at the end of one word and the beginning of the next word. The order of the letters may not be changed.

Example   The children had bats and balls.   *sand*

31 They are stored in his garage.   _____

32 Please collect all the books.   _____

33 Sally has gone with the rest.   _____

34 It is difficult to concentrate with all this noise.   _____

35 The ship rocks on the rough sea.   _____

Change the first word into the last word, by changing one letter at a time and making a new, different word in the middle.

Example   CASE *CASH* LASH

36 LAND _____ LEAD

37 NAIL _____ BALL

38 BOOT _____ HOST

39 CAME _____ COMB

40 SEND _____ SANG

Complete the following sentences by selecting the most sensible word from each group of words given in the brackets. Underline the words selected.

B 14

Example The (<u>children</u>, books, foxes) carried the (houses, <u>books</u>, steps) home from the (greengrocer, <u>library</u>, factory).

41 The (cats, birds, cows) (flew, burrowed, ran) to their (pool, den, nest).

42 The old lady (jumped, climbed, hopped) on to a (lorry, cycle, bus).

43 Please (colour, check, throw) your (change, book, ball) before you leave the (corridor, bedroom, shop).

44 The (dog, rider, footballer) (jumped, kicked, bit) the ball off the (horse, pitch, garden).

45 (Elephants, Rocks, Suitcases) have (stony, long, square) (mountains, handles, trunks).

5

Find and underline the two words which need to change places for each sentence to make sense.

B 17

Example She went to <u>letter</u> the <u>write</u>.

46 I there I could go wish.

47 I'll morning up early in the get.

48 Hide did you where the parcel?

49 He found the table on the book.

50 He over the ball threw the wall.

5

Fill in the missing letters. The alphabet has been written out to help you.

B 23

A B C D E F G H I J K L M N O P Q R S T U V W X Y Z

Example AB is to CD as PQ is to <u>RS</u>.

51 AC is to BD as MO is to _____.

52 ACE is to BDF as CEG is to _____.

53 AZ is to BY as CX is to _____.

54 ZX is to VT as SQ is to _____.

55 AG is to ZT as BH is to _____.

5

Fill in the crosswords so that all the given words are included. You have been given one letter as a clue in each crossword.

B 19

56–57

risky
seeds
every
taste
taper
piece

58–59

dirty
eaten
bears
bread
actor
sunny

4

3

Give the two missing groups of letters in the following sequences. The alphabet has been written out to help you.

B 23

A B C D E F G H I J K L M N O P Q R S T U V W X Y Z

Example   CQ   DP   EQ   FP   <u>GQ</u>   <u>HP</u>

60 AH   BI   CJ   DK   _____   _____

61 BA   DC   FE   HG   _____   _____

62 ZZA   YBY   XDW   WFU   _____   _____

63 GIH   IKJ   KML   MON   _____   _____

○ 4

Underline the two words, one from each group, which are closest in meaning.

B 3

Example   (race, shop, <u>start</u>)   (finish, <u>begin</u>, end)

64 (pale, dark, bulb)   (flower, light, day)

65 (leg, weapons, foot)   (hands, ankle, arms)

66 (before, connect, right)   (correct, wrong, left)

67 (lift, cushion, pillow)   (chair, protect, fight)

○ 4

68 If the code for TIME is 2786, what does 862 stand for? _____

B 24

69–71 If the code for TEASE is 84234, what do the following codes stand for?

284 _____   3428 _____   82384 _____

72 If the code for PURSE is 96483, what is the code for SUPPER? _____ .

○ 5

Underline the two words which are the odd ones out in the following groups of words.

B 4

Example   black   <u>king</u>   purple   green   <u>house</u>

73 stick   pipe   glue   heir   adhere

74 climb   ascend   mountain   hill   cliff

75 arrow   hedgehog   porcupine   pin   needle

76 attract   enchant   house   charm   bracelet

77 biscuit   flour   sugar   butter   cake

○ 5

If A = 1, B = 3, C = 4, D = 5, find the value of the following.

B 26

78 $(C - B) \times D =$ _____

79 $(D - A) + (B \times C) =$ _____

80 $D - (A + B) =$ _____

○ 3

Paper 2

Give the two missing pairs of letters in the following sequences. The alphabet has been written out to help you.

A B C D E F G H I J K L M N O P Q R S T U V W X Y Z

Example CQ   DP   EQ   FP   _GQ_   _HP_

1 NO   NP   _____   NR   _____   NT

2 JQ   KP   LO   MN   _____   _____

3 CN   EP   _____   IT   KV   _____

Here are the number codes for four words. Match the right code to the right word.

MAST   STAR   REST   TEA

5314   432   7214   1425

4 MAST   _____

5 STAR   _____

6 REST   _____

7 TEA   _____

8 Write REAM in code.   _____

Complete the following sentences by selecting the most sensible word from each group of words given in the brackets. Underline the words selected.

Example   The (children, books, foxes) carried the (houses, books, steps) home from the (greengrocer, library, factory).

9 He (kicked, chewed, painted) a (picture, door, dog) which was to hang in the (garden, street, classroom).

10 She (cooked, blocked, broke) the (vase, salad, weather) which had to be (put to bed, thrown away, bathed).

11 (Caterpillars, Flowers, Frogs) change into (petals, butterflies, tadpoles) with beautiful (wings, eyes, stems).

12 How many (add, divide, times) do I have to tell (me, you, tales) to close the (sum, sandwich, door) quietly!

13 The sun (rose, violet, tulip) over the horizon like a giant (green, orange, bouncy) (fish, flower, ball).

Underline two words, one from each group, that go together to form a new word. The word in the first group always comes first.

Example   (hand, <u>green</u>, for)   (light, <u>house</u>, sure)

14 (rock, face, band)   (age, worth, kind)

15 (be, was, do)   (age, hind, rear)

16 (life, birth, year)   (wrong, day, rear)

17 (silly, jester, fool)   (joke, hardy, fair)

18 (blue, colour, blush)   (more, gone, less)

5

Underline the one word in the brackets which will go equally well with both the pairs of words outside the brackets.

Example   rush, attack   cost, fee   (price, hasten, strike, <u>charge</u>, money)

19 overlook, lose   girl, lass   (more, miss, mark, drop, lose)

20 bright, well-lit   portable, easy to carry   (heavy, move, dark, light, glow)

21 cot, cradle   copy, forge   (crib, bed, stable, zoo, animals)

22 thread, string   fasten, tie   (lace, needle, pin, wire, bow)

23 timber, pole   glimmer, ray   (dark, light, shadow, beam, torch)

5

Find the letter which will end the first word and start the second word.

Example   peac (<u>h</u>) ome

24 wis   (_____)   elm

25 boo   (_____)   nee

26 gro   (_____)   ish

27 mea   (_____)   isp

28 sea   (_____)   rap

5

Look at the pair of words on the left. Underline the one word in the brackets that goes with the word outside the brackets in the same way as the first two words go together.

Example   good, better   bad, (naughty, worst, <u>worse</u>, nasty)

29 hinder, prevent   mean, (generous, spiteful, stop, involve)

30 inside, outside   above, (through, on, beyond, below)

31 closet, clot   parent, (part, rent, pant, trap)

32 hand, fingers   foot, (leg, sole, toes, arm)

33 quick, slowly   flat, (bumpy, unevenly, evenly, house)

5

Move one letter from the first word and add it to the second word to make two new words.

B 13

Example   hunt   sip   <u>hut</u>   <u>snip</u>

34 mend   raw   _____   _____

35 plump   and   _____   _____

36 clean   are   _____   _____

37 crave   cat   _____   _____

38 seal   bride   _____   _____

5

39–43 Look at these headings.

B 1

A	B	C
Musical instruments	Vegetables	Reptiles

Choose the correct group for each of the words below. Write in the letter.

turnip ___   bugle ___   adder ___   drum ___   cress ___   snake ___

piano ___   onion ___   tortoise ___   guitar ___

5

Find the three-letter word which can be added to the letters in capitals to make a new word. The new word will complete the sentence sensibly.

B 22

Example   The cat sprang onto the MO.   <u>USE</u>

44 Your front tyre has a CTURE.   _____

45 I have two SQUS and a rectangle.   _____

46 The flowers, which hadn't been WATE, were drooping.   _____

47 The washing, which had been BING in the wind, was quite dry.   _____

48 The GER climbed cautiously out of his sett.   _____

5

Find the four-letter word hidden at the end of one word and the beginning of the next word. The order of the letters may not be changed.

B 21

Example   The children had bats and balls.   <u>sand</u>

49 There are several pairs of shoes.   _____

50 Please climb into the cars now.   _____

51 The last three letters are there.   _____

52 The question is often asked.   _____

53 Soon the play will end.   _____

5

Find and underline the two words which need to change places for each sentence to make sense.

B 17

Example   She went to <u>letter</u> the <u>write</u>.

54 Mum was in cooking the kitchen.

55 We bus on the last went.

56 You can sums your do.

57 Cold think it is I today.

58 I got my all sums right.

5

Fill in the crosswords so that all the given words are included. You have been given one letter as a clue in each crossword.

B 19

59–60

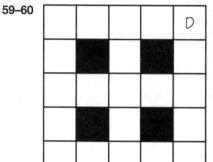

notes
reads
bread
doses
baron
exact

61–62

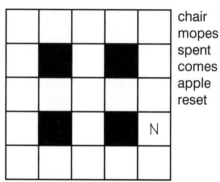

chair
mopes
spent
comes
apple
reset

4

Choose two words, one from each set of brackets, to complete the sentences in the best way.

B 15

Example   Smile is to happiness as (drink, <u>tear</u>, shout) is to (whisper, laugh, <u>sorrow</u>).

63 Green is to grass as (colour, blue, shade) is to (swim, sand, sky).

64 Food is to hunger as (drink, tea, coffee) is to (thirst, glass, wet).

65 Boy is to man as (girl, pupil, student) is to (school, niece, woman).

66 Top is to bottom as (over, high, aloft) is to (above, upper, low).

67 Well is to ill as (soft, silk, material) is to (heavy, hard, broken).

5

Give the two missing numbers in the following sequences.

B 23

Example   2 4 6 8 <u>10</u> <u>12</u>

68 18   13   9   ___   4   ___

69 ___   60   48   36   ___   12

70 3   8   14   21   ___   ___

71 ___   12   18   25   31   ___

72 11   13   12   ___   ___   17

5

A and B like blue.

C likes green but not red.

F likes red and green.

E only likes green.

B 25

73 Which colour is the most popular? _____

74 Which colour is the least popular? _____

75 How many more like blue than red? _____

76 How many only like one colour? _____

4

Rearrange the letters in capitals to make another word. The new word has something to do with the first two words.

B 16

Example	spot	soil	SAINT	_STAIN_
77 brute	savage	BASTE	_____
78 curl	circle	SPOOL	_____
79 weak	fragile	FLAIR	_____
80 letter	memo	STONE	_____

4

Now go to the Progress Chart to record your score!   Total   80

Paper 3

If the code for PURCHASE is £ + − × ÷ @ % /, what do these codes stand for?

B 24

  1 % ÷ @ − / %   _____   **2** % £ − + × /   _____

What are the codes for the following words?

  3 ARCHES _____   **4** SHARP _____   **5** CASH _____

5

Change one word so that the sentence makes sense. Underline the word you are taking out and write your new word on the line.

B 14

    Example   I waited in line to buy a <u>book</u> to see the film.   _ticket_

  6 After swimming we are sometimes allowed fish and towels for supper. _____

  7 The artist dipped his brush into the blue cream on his palette.   _____

  8 The train pulled into the supermarket and let the passengers get off.   _____

  9 Simon sharpened his ruler over the bin.   _____

10 The rain fell heavily against the door pane.   _____

5

Which one letter can be added to the front of all of these words to make new words?

B 12

> **Example**   _c_are   _c_at   _c_rate   _c_all

11 ___ance   ___ate   ___ash   ___art   ___one

12 ___are   ___lag   ___or   ___lash   ___eel

13 ___on   ___it   ___ant   ___as   ___edge

14 ___lank   ___loom   ___lock   ___lush   ___owl

15 ___ate   ___loss   ___rain   ___rind   ___utter

5

Change the first word of the third pair in the same way as the other pairs to give a new word.

B 18

> **Example**   bind, hind   bare, hare   but, <u>hut</u>

16 flat, that   flan, than   fling, _____

17 tiny, shiny   tatter, shatter   tell, _____

18 spot, tops   loot, tool   pots, _____

19 risk, whisk   rich, which   rose, _____

20 face, fire   space, spire   mace, _____

5

Underline the two words, one from each group, which are closest in meaning.

B 3

> **Example**   (race, shop, <u>start</u>)   (finish, <u>begin</u>, end)

21 (kidnap, take, hold)   (across, abduct, grab)

22 (fat, oil, butter)   (greasy, rich, lubricate)

23 (mean, scarce, merge)   (aged, scanty, solve)

24 (fruit, current, sweet)   (contemporary, cold, cherry)

25 (flabbergast, laugh, amusing)   (cry, flap, astound)

5

Underline the one word in the brackets which will go equally well with both the pairs of words outside the brackets.

B 5

> **Example**   rush, attack   cost, fee   (price, hasten, strike, <u>charge</u>, money)

26 shore, beach   freewheel, glide   (ocean, coast, rocks, cycle, sea)

27 animal, pet   pursue, follow   (wolf, dog, cat, cow, rat)

28 digit, number   form, shape   (whole, figure, set, mould, outline)

29 point, score   aim, target   (ambition, goal, match, game, team)

30 twig, bough   subdivision, offshoot   (root, leaflet, branch, learn, stem)

5

Complete the following sentences by selecting the most sensible word from each group of words given in the brackets. Underline the words selected.

Example The (<u>children</u>, books, foxes) carried the (houses, <u>books</u>, steps) home from the (greengrocer, <u>library</u>, factory).

31 The (boy, man, dog) (barked, shouted, cried) when he was put on a (walk, lead, foot).

32 Quickly, climb up the (dungeon, tower, door) and look at the (step, arrow, view).

33 (Lakes, Buildings, Forests) contain (flowers, trees, fish) where many types of (animal, mountain, boat) can make their homes.

34 Our class (teacher, computer, form captain) is always being used in project time to find (books, apples, information) from the Internet.

35 The boy walked (hungrily, quickly, badly) over the bridge so he had time to (play, work, colour) in the (feelings, puddles, smells) along the lane.

Complete the following sentences in the best way by choosing one word from each set of brackets.

Example Tall is to (tree, <u>short</u>, colour) as narrow is to (thin, white, <u>wide</u>).

36 Dawn is to (morning, night, sun) as (moon, light, dusk) is to evening.

37 Legs are to (jeans, feet, run) as (moles, wings, birds) are to fly.

38 Grass is to (green, meadow, cow) as sand is to (beach, castle, waves).

39 Day is to (seven, night, light) as month is to (spring, twelve, year).

40 (Hesitate, Depart, Stop) is to red as go is to (away, green, run).

Underline the pair of words most opposite in meaning.

Example cup, mug   coffee, milk   <u>hot, cold</u>

41 request, ask   misery, despair   refuse, offer

42 many, few   last, end   ally, helper

43 asleep, awake   plan, scheme   behaviour, conduct

44 ebb, flow   bad, evil   live, exist

45 remedy, cure   health, ailment   escape, getaway

Underline the two words which are the odd ones out in the following groups of words.

Example black   <u>king</u>   purple   green   <u>house</u>

46 pencil   instruction   lesson   teaching   pen

47 persuade   cajole   believe   coax   guess

48 pigsty   horse   trough   kennel   stable

49 bicycle   road   lorry   rail   bus

50 nephew   grandmother   sister   father   daughter

Find a word that can be put in front of each of the following words to make new, compound words.

Example   cast   fall   ward   pour   _down_

51 draw   stand   hold   out   _____

52 piece   mind   class   work   _____

53 care   noon   effect shock   _____

54 stairs   set   right   hill   _____

55 fall   cap   dress   light   _____

Fill in the crosswords so that all the given words are included. You have been given one letter as a clue in each crossword.

56–57

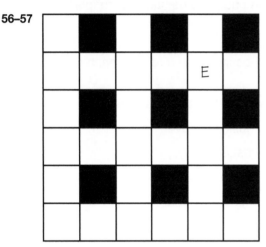

turkey, uglier, angles, carpet,
points, settee

58–59

etched, aspect, advert, praise,
choice, storms

Give the two missing numbers in the following sequences.

Example   2 4 6 8 _10_ _12_

60 8   9   11   14   ___   23   ___

61 108   ___   84   72   60   48   ___

62 74   60   48   ___   ___   24   20

63 11   ___   12   15   ___   17   14

64 ___   2   5   4   6   ___   7

The twins are having a party on 30 December, Gary's party is three days later, but Cathy is having hers a week before the twins.

65 What day is Gary's party on?   _____

66 What day is Cathy's party on?   _____

67 The twins have to postpone their party for a fortnight. It is now on _____.

If these words were placed in alphabetical order:

B 20

    douse   double   down   doubt   dough

68 which word would be last? _____

69 which word would be first? _____

70 If the words were written backwards, which would be the last in alphabetical order? _____

3

Find the letter which will complete both pairs of words, ending the first word and starting the second. The same letter must be used for both pairs of words.

B 10

Example   mea ($\underline{t}$) able   fi ($\underline{t}$) ub

71 tea (__) isk   pur (__) ope   **72** pa (__) ork   pillo (__) eather

73 bul (__) arge   bar (__) ush   **74** was (__) ear   sli (__) ond

75 crow (__) od   pla (__) oon

5

Find the four-letter word hidden at the end of one word and the beginning of the next word. The order of the letters may not be changed.

B 21

Example   The children had bats and balls.   <u>sand</u>

76 He keeps the stamps from envelopes.   _____

77 Mistakes can be easily made.   _____

78 She grew inky-blue flowers in the garden.   _____

79 It's your turn after mine.   _____

80 He replied angrily, and ran out.   _____

5

Now go to the Progress Chart to record your score!   Total   80

Paper 4

Look at the first group of three words. The word in the middle has been made from the other two words. Complete the second group of three words in the same way, making a new word in the middle.

B 18

    Example   PAIN INTO TOOK   ALSO <u>SOON</u> ONLY

1 KERB BARK ASKS   AJAR _____ EELS

2 PITY TYPE PEAS   BONE _____ STIR

3 TAIL WAIT THAW   SOUR _____ LEAF

4 ENDS DICE ICED   SOBS _____ EDGE

5 TINS BIND DRAB   WOOD _____ KILT

5

Find the three-letter word which can be added to the letters in capitals to make a new word. The new word will complete each sentence sensibly.

B 22

Example The cat sprang onto the MO.   <u>USE</u>

6 They listen when the teacher SKS. _____

7 I like HY on my toast. _____

8 The WHER was very cold. _____

9 He enjoyed PING in the sand. _____

10 The house was now VAT. _____

5

Underline two words, one from each group, that go together to form a new word. The word in the first group always comes first.

B 8

Example (hand, <u>green</u>, for)   (light, <u>house</u>, sure)

11 (there, which, when)   (was, time, fore)

12 (far, near, out)   (hold, law, police)

13 (in, an, it)   (soft, side, right)

14 (leg, hand, saw)   (some, ankle, kick)

15 (top, cap, hat)   (tile, able, list)

5

Add one letter to the word in capital letters to make a new word. The meaning of the new word is given in the clue.

B 12

Example PLAN   simple   <u>plain</u>

16 REVERE   to turn round   _____

17 WING   to squeeze   _____

18 PEAK   to say something   _____

19 PACE   quietness   _____

20 SOON   eating utensil   _____

5

Give the two missing numbers in the following sequences.

B 23

Example 2 4 6 8 <u>10</u> <u>12</u>

21	2	4	7	11	16	___	29	___
22	35	44	46	55	57	66	___	___
23	3	6	7	___	11	14	___	18
24	___	4	12	11	33	32	96	___
25	80	___	76	71	72	67	___	63

5

Underline the two words which are the odd ones out in the following groups of words.

Example black <u>king</u> purple green <u>house</u>

26 call   rain   frost   whisper   snow

27 book   see   view   programme   watch

28 colour   face   tint   leg   hue

29 write   draw   animal   print   house

30 skin   banana   apple   jelly   peach

B 4

5

Find the relationship between these letters and numbers.

Example AB is to CD as PQ is to <u>RS</u>.

31 AE is to BF and MR is to NS as LP is to _____.

32 12 is to 36 and 9 is to 27 as 17 is to _____.

33 81 is to 27 and 54 is to 18 as 93 is to _____.

34 49 is to 7 and 1 is to 1 as 81 is to _____.

35 1000 is to 10 and 10 is to 0.1 as 10,000 is to _____.

B 23

5

If the code for CLOTHES is ▲ ❑ ■ ▼ ○ ● ◆, what do the following codes stand for?

36 ◆ ■ ■ ▼ ○ ●   _____

37 ▲ ❑ ■ ◆ ●   _____

38 ❑ ■ ◆ ▼   _____

What are the codes for the following words?

39 THOSE   _____

40 HOST   _____

B 24

5

Underline the pair of words most opposite in meaning.

Example cup, mug   coffee, milk   <u>hot, cold</u>

41 warm, balmy   fire, ice   burn, flame

42 bed, time   snow, ball   freeze, heat

43 dawn, daybreak   night, morning   milk, bottle

44 sea, land   buy, purchase   bathe, paddle

45 snow, cold   sun, shine   toil, rest

B 9

5

Underline the one word in the brackets which will go equally well with both the pairs of words outside the brackets.

Example rush, attack   cost, fee   (pricel, hasten, strike, <u>charge</u>, money)

46 blackout, giddy   faded, unclear   (fast, ill, faint, well, pure)

47 gale, blast   upset, calamity   (strike, luck, blow, feel, wind)

48 attract, please   spell, magic   (charm, mascot, wizard, interest, draw)

49 chief, main   money, wealth   (town, bank, capital, cash, credit)

50 split, shatter   interval, holiday   (vacation, pause, break, splinter, crumble)

5

Rearrange the muddled words in capital letters so that each sentence makes sense.

Example There are sixty SNODCES <u>seconds</u> in a UTMINE <u>minute</u>.

51 A GNILLOR _____ stone gathers no SOMS _____.

52 There are NEVES _____ days in a KEWE _____.

53 Don't UTNOC _____ your SKINECCH _____ before they are hatched.

54 Cardiff is the TPCAIAL _____ of LESAW _____.

55 There are EVNES _____ colours in the WBRAION _____.

5

Solve the problem by working out the letter code. The alphabet has been written out to help you.

A B C D E F G H I J K L M N O P Q R S T U V W X Y Z

Example If the code for SECOND is written as UGEQPF, what is the code for THIRD? <u>VJKTF</u>

56 If the code for TIME is ODHZ, what is the code for CLOCK? _____

57 If the code for SHADOW is HSZWLD, what is the code for SUNLIGHT?_____

58 If the code for PINK is QJOL, what is the code for BLUE? _____

59 If the code for BASKET is CBTLFU, what does TUVC mean? _____

60 If the code for STUDY is QRSBW, what does BSQR mean? _____

5

Fill in the crosswords so that all the given words are included. You have been given one letter as a clue in each crossword.

61–62

potter, nettle, sicken, astute, sprays, static

63–64

opened, hoping, intend, greets, peanut, kettle

4

If these words were placed in alphabetical order:

65 baby   school-girl   student   grown-up   pensioner

Which word would be first? _____

66 seed   seedling   leaf   bud   flower

Which word would be last? _____

67 pram   pushchair   tricycle   bicycle   car

Which word would be fourth? _____

68 letter   word   sentence   paragraph   book

Which word would be second? _____

69 none   single   triple   quadruple   double

Which word would be third? _____

5

Read the first two statements and then underline one of the four options below that must be true.

70 'People are animals. Animals are not wood.'

Some animals are kept as pets.

People build with wood.

People are not wood.

A dog is a type of animal.

1

17

Find the two letters which will end the first word and start the second word.

B 10

Example   rea (c h) air

71 chis   (___ ___) dest   72 hand (___ ___) ad

73 chan   (___ ___) ese   74 met   (___ ___) most

75 cent   (___ ___) ad

5

Find and underline the two words which need to change places for each sentence to make sense.

B 17

Example   She went to <u>letter</u> the <u>write</u>.

76 Your is where big sister?

77 My need all pencils sharpening.

78 Some made I scones today.

79 I at having my lunch like school.

80 I take my day out each dog.

5

Now go to the Progress Chart to record your score!   Total   80

Paper 5

Find a word that is similar in meaning to the word in capital letters and that rhymes with the second word.

B 5

Example   CABLE   tyre   <u>wire</u>

1 ENEMY   doe   _____

2 SUCCESSOR   care   _____

3 UNEVEN   stuff   _____

4 PEACEFUL   harm   _____

5 CENTRE   fiddle   _____

5

Complete the following sentences in the best way by choosing one word from each set of brackets.

B 15

Example   Tall is to (tree, <u>short</u>, colour) as narrow is to (thin, white, <u>wide</u>).

6 Jug is to (pour, milk, measure) as glass is to (clear, water, window).

7 Leave is to (come, tree, drop) as part is to (join, piece, act).

8 Fish is to (chips, water, scales) as bird is to (burgers, beak, feathers).

9 Yours is to (hers, its, you) as mine is to (coal, me, them).

10 Conventional is to (odd, easy, worried) as abnormal is to (unusual, peculiar, normal).

5

Underline the one word in the brackets which will go equally well with both the pairs of words outside the brackets.

Example   rush, attack   cost, fee   (price, hasten, strike, <u>charge</u>, money)

11 solid, lump   obstacle, stop   (hard, block, firm, halt, shape)

12 charge, price   meal, food   (feed, cost, fare, do, supper)

13 clip, trim   yield, produce   (crop, cut, scissors, farm, tidy)

14 column, pole   position, assignment   (cancel, job, post, stamp, appointment)

15 brain, head   resent, dislike   (top, hate, mind, care, bother)

Find the missing number that makes the sum makes sense.

Example $6 \times 2 = \underline{4} + 8$

16 ___ $+ 12 = 7 \times 6$

17 $9 \times 9 = 11 +$ ___ $+ 12$

18 $14 \div$ ___ $= 10 - 8$

19 $14 + 16 =$ ___ $- 13 - 4$

20 $5 \times 2 = 20 \div$ ___ $+ 6$

Underline the one word which **cannot be made** from the letters of the word in capital letters.

Example   STATIONERY   stone tyres ration <u>nation</u> noisy

21 DREAD   dear   bad   red   dead   dare

22 SPATTER   reap   treat   sprat   tease   spear

23 CREMATE   mace   cream   tamer   crate   matter

24 CARPENTER   truce   creep   preen   prance   carpet

25 DISTEMPER   strim   stems   temper   demise   pester

Underline two words, one from each group, that go together to form a new word. The word in the first group always comes first.

Example   (hand, <u>green</u>, for)   (light, <u>house</u>, sure)

26 (high, fight, road)   (shout, noise, light)

27 (rung, rang, ring)   (out, let, off)

28 (ticket, fare, bus)   (punch, gone, well)

29 (under, over, next)   (board, cloth, bored)

30 (cross, tick, ring)   (test, right, bow)

Find the four-letter word hidden at the end of one word and the beginning of the next word. The order of the letters may not be changed.

B 21

Example   The children had bats and balls.   sand

31 We tried to urge our team to win.   _____

32 Out of breath, the last rower lent over his oar.   _____

33 'Which information is correct?' queried the teacher.   _____

34 When you are seated, please attach the safety belt.   _____

35 For old people, climbing steps can be difficult.   _____

5

Remove one letter from the word in capital letters to leave a new word. The meaning of the new word is given in the clue.

B 12

Example   AUNT   an insect   ant

36 SPORTED   arranged   _____

37 HEAVEN   harbour   _____

38 MINDED   dug out of the ground   _____

39 SPRINT   a kind of writing   _____

40 BRIDGE   a woman on her wedding day   _____

5

Complete the following sentences by selecting the most sensible word from each group of words given in the brackets. Underline the words selected.

B 14

Example   The (<u>children</u>, books, foxes) carried the (houses, <u>books</u>, steps) home from the (greengrocer, <u>library</u>, factory).

41 The (car, train, plane) which was travelling in the fast (runway, lane, road) swerved and hit a (pilot, wheel, pedestrian).

42 Please take your (books, marbles, sandwiches) off the teacher's (car, desk, fridge) as you will need them for the next (door, lesson, breakfast).

43 '(Sweets, Blue, Flowers) is my favourite (chocolate, vase, colour)', she said kindly, unwrapping the home-made (scarf, puppy, plant).

44 The police arrived quickly at the (site, ground, scene) of the accident, as they were only a few (years, streets, towns) away.

45 Under cover of (blankets, darkness, trees) the (lioness, baby, thief) climbed through the warehouse (jungle, window, bed).

5

Fill in the missing letters. The alphabet has been written out to help you.

A B C D E F G H I J K L M N O P Q R S T U V W X Y Z

Example AB is to CD as PQ is to RS.

46 AE is to CG as IM is to **KO**.

47 AZB is to BYC as CXD is to **DWE**.

48 EJG is to GLA as INJ is to **KPD**.

49 BDB is to DFD as FHF is to **HJH**.

50 RH is to PJ as ND is to **LF**.

B 23

5

Change the first word into the last word, by changing one letter at a time and making two new, different words in the middle.

Example CASE CASH WASH WISH

51 DEAR ___ ___ BEST

52 BEND ___ ___ TANK

53 FOAL ___ ___ FARM

54 POTS ___ ___ PAST

55 HARD ___ ___ KIND

B 13

5

Fill in the crosswords so that all the given words are included. You have been given one letter as a clue in each crossword.

56–57

		M

ham, men, den, ore,
are, hod

58–59

	L	

hoe, ash, leo, ale,
ewe, sew

B 19

4

Give the two missing numbers in the following sequences.

Example 2 4 6 8 10 12

60 12   15   ___   30   42   ___   75

61 7   ___   9   16   11   24   ___

62 ___   93   86   ___   72   65   58

B 23

3

21

Change one word so that the sentence makes sense. Underline the word you are taking out and write your new word on the line.

B 14

Example   I waited in line to buy a <u>book</u> to see the film.   *ticket*

63 Mia's bike had a flat saddle.   _____

64 As the sun set in the east, Ali watched the shadows lengthen.   _____

65 The high grass that surrounded the castle was designed to keep out the enemy.   _____

66 I find it difficult to thread my cushion in my sewing lessons.   _____

67 Take a tissue and blow your trumpet rather than sniff.   _____

5

If the code for APPEARANCE is @ = = X @ £ @ + ÷ X, what do the following codes stand for?

B 24

68 ÷ @ = X   _____

69 @ £ X   _____

What are the codes for the following words?

70 PREEN   _____

71 NEAR   _____

72 PRANCE   _____

5

Rearrange the letters in capitals to make another word. The new word has something to do with the first two words.

B 16

Example   spot   soil   SAINT   <u>STAIN</u>

73 law   regulation   LURE   _____

74 bandage   gauze   STAPLER   _____

75 cheer   gladden   ASLEEP   _____

76 believe   depend   STRUT   _____

77 sea   water   CANOE   _____

5

If A = 2, B = 3, C = 4, D = 5, E = 6, F = 7, L = 8, N = 9, find the sum of the following words.

B 26

78 faded   _____

79 clean   _____

80 bleed   _____

3

Now go to the Progress Chart to record your score!   Total   **80**

Paper 6

If E = 5, I = 6, P = 8, N = 4, S = 10, R = 12, T = 20, find the sum of the following words.

1 stripe _____

2 rinse _____

3 prints _____

4 spinner _____

5 trip _____

○ 5

Rearrange the letters in capitals to make another word. The new word has something to do with the first two words.

	Example	spot	soil	SAINT	_STAIN_
6	wrong	incorrect		FLEAS	_____
7	snares	catches		SPRAT	_____
8	copy	draw		CRATE	_____
9	broom	mop		SHRUB	_____
10	diagram	chart		BLEAT	_____
11	saying	expression		SERAPH	_____

○ 6

Find the four-letter word hidden at the end of one word and the beginning of the next word. The order of the letters may not be changed.

Example   The children had bats and balls.   _sand_

12 They were all caught in a rainstorm.   _____

13 He hoped that something would turn up.   _____

14 The youngest toddler cried for his mother.   _____

15 Luckily their delays were not too lengthy.   _____

16 I want to run in the race for the charity.   _____

○ 5

Complete the following sentences by selecting the most sensible word from each group of words given in the brackets. Underline the words selected.

Example   The (<u>children</u>, books, foxes) carried the (houses, <u>books</u>, steps) home from the (greengrocer, <u>library</u>, factory).

17 The (TV, trellis, terrace) was covered with (rhubarb, rubbish, roses) which needed (planting, pointing, pruning).

18 The (weather, book, cardigan) was so (exciting, uninteresting, chilly) she did not want to put it (down, up, out).

19 The hailstones (drummed, whistled, smoked) on the (chimney, car roof, carpet) as they were driving to (winter, school, distraction).

20 The (savage, docile, tender) dog bit the (fireman, electrician, postman) as he was delivering the (milk, letters, pigeons).

21 He would have to choose the right time of (night, year, day) to (wrestle, water, whistle) the (pillars, plants, penguins).

Find the two letters which will end the first word and start the second word.

Example   rea (c h) air

22 purp   (— —) ague

23 bran   (— —) arge

24 peri   (— —) ield

25 mosa (— —) icle

26 fast   (— —) gine

Give the two missing groups of letters or numbers in the following sequences. The alphabet has been written out to help you with numbers 27 and 28.

A B C D E F G H I J K L M N O P Q R S T U V W X Y Z

Example   CQ   DP   EQ   FP   *GQ*   *HP*

27	——	BF	CG	DH	——	FJ	
28	ZK	YL	——	WN	VO	——	
29	3Z8	——	5V6	——	7R4	8P3	
30	A3	A4	——	B9	——	C18	D24
31	7	15	9	17	——	——	

Underline the pair of words most similar in meaning.

Example   come, go   roam, wander   fear, fare

32 remember, forget   rest, work   rival, opponent

33 rise, fall   spine, backbone   half, whole

34 recoup, revolve   sure, certain   straight, crooked

35 bluff, pretend   before, after   believe, distrust

36 noise, silence   fair, dark   brave, fearless

24

Underline the two words in each line which are made from the same letters.

    Example   TAP   PET   <u>TEA</u>   POT   <u>EAT</u>

37 TEST   NEST   WENT   TENS   TENT

38 STEP   STAY   TAME   MAZE   PEST

39 PEEP   LEAP   PALE   SLAP   PLAY

40 WEST   REST   STIR   WIRE   STEW

41 LEER   LAIR   REAL   RAIL   RULE

      5

Find and underline the two words which need to change places for each sentence to make sense.

    Example   She went to <u>letter</u> the <u>write</u>.

42 There in a funny smell was the kitchen.

43 I was three was my sister when born.

44 He brave a very was man.

45 She into the flour sieved a bowl.

46 We start soon will school.

      5

The word TEACHER is written in code as   ▷ ~ ○ ● ▮ ~ ■
Decode these words.

47 ● ▮ ~ ○ ▷   _____

48 ○ ● ▮ ~   _____

49 ▷ ■ ○ ● ~   _____

Write these words in code.

50 CRATE   _____

51 ARCH   _____

      5

Find the three-letter word which can be added to the letters in capitals to make a new word. The new word will complete the sentence sensibly.

    Example   The cat sprang onto the MO. <u>USE</u>

52 They SED at the amazing sight.   _____

53 He HD the cry of the owl to its mate.   _____

54 He stuck his GUE out at the boy.   _____

55 The lion RED.   _____

56 It was an AE angle.   _____

      5

Underline two words, one from each group, that go together to form a new word. The word in the first group always comes first.

Example   (hand, <u>green</u>, for)   (light, <u>house</u>, sure)

57 (glass, cup, food)   (shelf, floor, board)

58 (check, tick, cross)   (down, side, word)

59 (by, side, fore)   (ground, paper, wall)

60 (live, healthy, dead)   (key, well, lock)

61 (flood, for, furniture)   (give, away, breakage)

5

Find the missing number by using the two numbers outside the brackets in the same way as the other sets of numbers.

Example   2 [8] 4   3 [18] 6   5 [25] 5

62 9 [11] 2   7 [12] 5   8 [__] 6

63 3 [5] 15   5 [6] 30   8 [__] 24

64 2 [7] 3   6 [19] 7   4 [__] 7

65 8 [18] 9   3 [8] 4   6 [__] 1

66 5 [10] 4   6 [12] 4   9 [__] 2

5

Anne and Emma learn ballroom dancing and judo.
Emma and Lucy learn judo and fencing.
Caroline and Anne learn tap dancing and ballroom dancing.

67 Who learns judo but not fencing?   _____

68 Who learns ballroom dancing but not tap dancing?   _____

69 Which activity doesn't Anne learn?   _____

70 Which activity doesn't Emma learn?   _____

71 How many girls do three activities?   _____

5

Change the first word into the last word, by changing one letter at a time and making two new, different words in the middle.

Example   CASE   <u>CASH</u>   <u>WASH</u>   WISH

72 TAKE   _____   _____   LIVE

73 PIPE   _____   _____   HILL

74 GOOD   _____   _____   WORK

75 COSY   _____   _____   MIST

76 BLOW   _____   _____   BOAT

5

Imagine each of these words spelled backwards, then write the number below each word to indicate if it would be 1st, 2nd, 3rd or 4th in alphabetical order.

B 20

77 FATTEN   LIGHTEN   MOISTEN   SOFTEN

_____   _____   _____   _____

78 COMICAL   FINAL   MUSICAL   OFFICIAL

_____   _____   _____   _____

79 CATCHMENT   FITMENT   ODDMENT   SEGMENT

_____   _____   _____   _____

80 DANCING   CRYING   FLYING   SAYING

_____   _____   _____   _____

4

Now go to the Progress Chart to record your score!   Total   80

Paper 7

Underline the two words which are made from the same letters.

B 7

	Example	TAP	PET	<u>TEA</u>	POT	<u>EAT</u>
1	NEED	SEND	MEND	DINS	DENS	PRICE
2	STEM	LOTS	LAST	MIND	MAST	SALT
3	LAPSE	LIMPS	LAMPS	LUMPS	SEPAL	PULSE
4	SPACE	ADDER	STING	DREAD	START	TINTS
5	POST	PORT	POND	PEST	PACK	STOP

5

Move one letter from the first word and add it to the second word to make two new words.

B 13

Example   hunt   sip   *hut*   *snip*

6 trust   rend   _____   _____

7 prose   lace   _____   _____

8 front   ice   _____   _____

9 clean   plan   _____   _____

10 beat   end   _____   _____

5

27

Complete the following sentences in the best way by choosing one word from each set of brackets.

B 15

Example Tall is to (tree, <u>short</u>, colour) as narrow is to (thin, white, <u>wide</u>).

11 Pull is to (row, push, run) as out is to (door, down, in).

12 Lean is to (tilt, bumpy, hungry) as flat is to (level, uneven, tall).

13 Chicken is to (grain, coop, egg) as grass is to (seed, green, hay).

14 Adore is to (cherish, dislike, ignore) as doubt is to (question, remember, answer).

15 Ruin is to (build, help, destroy) as find is to (buy, borrow, discover).

5

These number codes match three of the four words given, but you are not told which code matches which word.

B 24

3844	6851	3824	
BALL	WAIL	BASE	WALL

Write the correct code next to each word.

16 BALL _____   17 WAIL _____

18 BASE _____   19 WALL _____

Decode this number:

20 4835 _____

5

Underline the word in the brackets closest in meaning to the word in capitals.

B 5

Example UNHAPPY (unkind death laughter <u>sad</u> friendly)

21 HAMMER (shout call mallet strike hurt)

22 ELASTIC (ribbon flexible hard clothes wider)

23 HUNGRY (tired listless thirsty ravenous bad)

24 WHOLE (entire part section sector big)

25 WASH (wait soap cleanse towel brush)

5

Change one word so that the sentence makes sense. Underline the word you are taking out and write your new word on the line.

B 14

Example I waited in line to buy a <u>book</u> to see the film. *ticket*

26 'Happy thirteenth holidays, Warren', shouted his mother. _____

27 The cat took her bone to her kennel and quietly ate it. _____

28 The soldier waved at her subjects as she stood on the balcony at Buckingham Palace. _____

29 Jamil carefully took down a heavy reference picture from the library shelf and started to read. _____

30 Our newts grew legs and turned into frogs. _____

5

Find the three-letter word which can be added to the letters in capitals to make a new word. The new word will complete the sentence sensibly.

B 22

Example   The cat sprang onto the MO.   <u>USE</u>

31 He put the SLE on the horse.   _____

32 Where do they SD for the ceremony?   _____

33 Mum likes CUSD on her fruit.   _____

34 The cook put CURTS in the cake.   _____

35 TE are her books.   _____

5

Give the two missing numbers in the following sequences.

B 23

Example   2   4   6   8   <u>10</u>   <u>12</u>

36	77	70	___	56	49	___		
37	38	41	45	___	___	63		
38	2	___	8	16	___	64		
39	5	16	10	14	15	12	___	___
40	80	33	90	39	___	___	110	51

5

Find the two letters which will end the first word and start the second word.

B 10

Example   rea (c h) air

41 almo   (___ ___) ance

42 tren   (___ ___) arge

43 broa   (___ ___) eap

44 cri   (___ ___) ge

45 ash   (___ ___) joy

5

Solve the problem by working out the letter code. The alphabet has been written out to help you.

B 24

A B C D E F G H I J K L M N O P Q R S T U V W X Y Z

Example   If the code for SECOND is UGEQPF, what is the code for THIRD?   <u>VJKTF</u>

46 If the code for FLEET is 17336, what is the code for LEFT?   _____

47 If the code for PILLOW is QHMKPV, what is the code for BLANKET?   _____

48 If the code for HARD is JCTF, what is the code for SOFT?   _____

49 If the code for BLACK is AKZBJ, what does ROKZRG mean?   _____

50 If the code for HANDY is JCPFA, what is the code for LUMP?   _____

5

Underline one word in the brackets which is most opposite in meaning to the word in capitals.

| | **Example** | WIDE | (broad | vague | long | <u>narrow</u> | motorway) |

51	TUTOR	(trainer	instructor	teacher	pupil	master)
52	END	(finish	commence	completion	conclusion	last)
53	TIE	(loosen	unite	fasten	join	clasp)
54	CLIMB	(ascend	rise	increase	descend	grow)
55	SHOW	(exhibition	reveal	hide	count	display)

○ 5

Find a word that can be put in front of each of the following words to make new, compound words.

| | **Example** | cast | fall | ward | pour | *down* |

56	weight	back	work	clip	_____
57	attack	sign	act	part	_____
58	take	stand	wear	water	_____
59	gear	lamp	phones	line	_____
60	weed	side	front	food	_____

○ 5

Fill in the crosswords so that all the given words are included. You have been given one letter as a clue in each crossword.

61–62

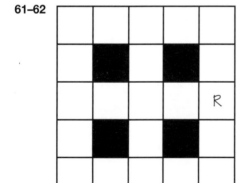

early, solid, spare, daddy,
later, acted

63–64

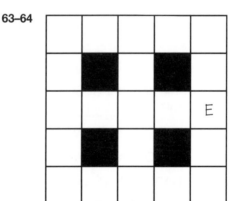

evens, await, super, stale,
rates, peace

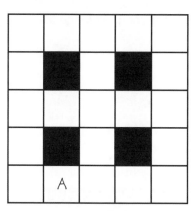

65-66

opera, eases, dimly, meets, drone, years

FURROW   FUSE   FURNITURE   FUSS   FURNACE

If these words were put in alphabetical order which one would come:

67 first   _____   **68** last   _____

69 in the middle _____   **70** fourth _____

71 second   _____

At a riding stables, five stables were empty and five had horses in them. The empty stables are shaded in this diagram.

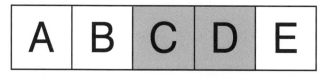

The five horses were:

Beauty   Trigger   Willow   Emily   Halo

Beauty was in the stable next to Halo. Trigger was next to Emily. Trigger was opposite Beauty. Halo was not on the same side as Willow.

Use this information to say which horse was in these stables:

72 A _____   **73** B _____   **74** E _____

75 G _____   **76** H _____

6

B 20

5

B 25

5

Find and underline the two words which need to change places for each sentence to make sense.

B 17

Example   She went to <u>letter</u> the <u>write</u>.

77 Is Tuesday it or Wednesday tomorrow?

78 Please may I room the leave?

79 Twenty-four four six times is.

80 Fur is as soft as cat's silk.

4

Now go to the Progress Chart to record your score!   Total   80

Paper 8

Underline the two words, one from each group, which are closest in meaning.

B 3

Example   (race, shop, <u>start</u>)   (finish, <u>begin</u>, end)

1 (water, pit, trap)   (door, fall, snare)

2 (borrow, let, rent)   (flat, allow, own)

3 (too, pear, seventh)   (also, two, heaven)

4 (bowl, field, town)   (bat, dish, country)

5 (watch, measure, sea)   (time, survey, shore)

5

Find and underline the two words which need to change places for each sentence to make sense.

B 17

Example   She went to <u>letter</u> the <u>write</u>.

6 Is too bath your hot?

7 I may it think snow today.

8 Did at leave it you the club?

9 I've her to meet got at 1 o'clock.

10 I put on book the the shelf.

5

If the code for SURGEON is 4783652, what are the codes for the following words?

B 24

11 SOON _____   12 GONE _____

13 ROSE _____   14 OURS _____

What does this code stand for?

15 27846 _____

5

1–5 Category A contains words to do with illnesses (**fever, cough**)
Category B contains words to do with complexion (**clear, tanned**)
Category C contains words that are fruits (**currant, damson**)
Category D contains words that are vegetables (**sprouts, bean**)
Category E contains words that are animals (**ewe, pony**)

6 warm 'Cool' means moderately cold so 'warm', which means moderately hot, is the most opposite in meaning. 'Hot' is a more extreme temperature than 'cool', so it is not correct.

7 precise 'Inaccurate' means incorrect so 'precise', which means exact, is the most opposite in meaning.

8 complicated 'Simple' means easy or uncomplicated, so 'complicated' is the most opposite in meaning.

9 hinder 'Assist' means to help or aid, so 'hinder', which means to hold back, is the most opposite in meaning.

10 last 'Initial' means first, so 'last' is the most opposite in meaning.

11 sweet Sugar and honey both taste sweet; 'sweet' is another name for a dessert or pudding.

12 flat A flat is an apartment; 'flat' also means level or even.

13 spot 'Spot' is another word for a speck or stain; it also means to see or to notice.

14 mug A mug holds liquid, like a pot or a cup; 'mug' can also mean to attack or beat up someone.

15 flag 'Flag' is another word for a pennant or banner; 'to flag', is to tire or to become exhausted.

16 d kind, desk
17 t fist, tool
18 k link, kind
19 n oxen, nail
20 e bore, east

21–25 Solve these questions by looking at the first set of three and working out how the first and last numbers have been used to arrive at the middle number. Apply this to the second set of three and see if it works. If it does, apply it to the last set.

21 14 $7 + 5 = 12$ and $3 + 8 = 11$, so $5 + 9 = 14$
22 6 $20 \div 4 = 5$ and $16 \div 4 = 4$, so $18 \div 3 = 6$
23 17 $7 + 4 + 2 = 13$ and $3 + 2 + 2 = 7$, so $6 + 9 + 2 = 17$

24 10 $(8 \times 3) \div 2 = 12$ and $(6 \times 6) \div 2 = 18$, so $(5 \times 4) \div 2 = 10$
25 2 $9 - 2 - 2 = 5$ and $8 - 5 - 2 = 1$, so $11 - 7 - 2 = 2$
26 forgot
27 overtake
28 underground
29 fingerprint
30 below
31 rest They <u>are st</u>ored in his garage.
32 tall Please collec<u>t all</u> the books.
33 here Sally has gone wit<u>h the re</u>st.
34 hall It is difficult to concentrate wit<u>h all</u> this noise.
35 hero The ship rocks on t<u>he ro</u>ugh sea.
36 LEND
37 BAIL
38 HOOT
39 COME
40 SAND

41–45 Try each of the words in the first set of brackets. Do they make sense with any words in the second and third set of brackets? Only one combination of three words makes sense.

41 birds, flew, nest
42 climbed, bus
43 check, change, shop
44 footballer, kicked, pitch
45 Elephants, long, trunks
46 I **wish** I could go **there**.
47 I'll **get** up early in the **morning**.
48 Where did you **hide** the parcel?
49 He **found** the **book** on the table.
50 He **threw** the ball **over** the wall.
51 NP Each letter in the first pair moves forward by one letter in the second pair.
52 DFH Each letter in the first trio moves forward by one letter in the second trio.
53 DW The first letter in the first pair moves forward by one letter and the second letter in the pair moves back by one letter.
54 OM Each letter in the first pair moves back by four letters in the second pair.
55 YS This is a mirror pair, where the two letters are an equal distance from the centre of the alphabet. Y is the mirror pair to B and S is the mirror pair to H.

56–57

T	A	P	E	R
A		I		I
S	E	E	D	S
T		C		K
E	V	E	R	Y

EXPANDED ANSWERS

B	E	A	R	S
R	■	C	■	U
E	A	T	E	N
A	■	O	■	N
D	I	R	T	Y

60 **EL, FM** Each letter in a pair moves forward by one letter in the following pair.

61 **JI, LK** Both of the letters in each pair move forward by two letters each time.

62 **VHS, UJQ** The first letter in each trio moves back by one letter each time, the second letter moves forward by two letters each time and the third letter moves back by two letters each time. (After Z the next letter will be A as the alphabet will start again.)

63 **OQP, QSR** Each letter in the trio moves forward by two letters each time.

64 **pale, light** Both words mean having a subtle colour.

65 **weapons, arms** Both words are used for implements that can be used to injure or kill.

66 **right, correct** Both words mean true or accurate.

67 **cushion, protect** Both words mean to shield from danger.

68 **MET** If the code is T = 2, I = 7, M = 8, E = 6 then 862 = MET.

69–71 **ATE, SEAT, TASTE** If the code is 8 = T, 4 = E, 2 = A, 3 = S and 4 = E, then 284 = ATE, 3428 = SEAT and 82384 = TASTE.

72 **869934** If the code is P = 9, U = 6, R = 4, S = 8, E = 3 then SUPPER = 869934.

73 **pipe, heir** The other three words all mean fasten or bond together.

74 **climb, ascend** The other three words are all natural features.

75 **hedgehog, porcupine** The other three words are all things, not animals, with a sharp point.

76 **house, bracelet** The other three words all mean to fascinate.

77 **biscuit, cake** The other three words are all ingredients, not ready-made bakes.

78–80 To complete this type of question, follow the rules of BIDMAS: complete the brackets first, then the multiplication or division and finally the addition or subtraction.

78 **5** (4 – 3) = 1, so 1 × 5 = 5

79 **16** (5 – 1) = 4 and (3 × 4) = 12.
4 + 12 = 16

80 **1** (1 + 3) = 4, so 5 – 4 = 1

Paper 2 (pages 5–9)

1 **NQ, NS** The first letter in each pair stays the same. The second letter moves forward by one letter each time.

2 **NM, OL** The first letter in each pair moves forward by one letter each time. The second letter moves back by one letter each time.

3 **GR, MX** Each letter in the pair moves forward by two letters each time.

4–8 Start with TEA, as that is the only three-letter word, so it is easy to match it to the correct code. That tells you that 4 = T, 3 = E and 2 = A. Knowing these three number and letter pairings will allow you to work out the rest.

4 **7214** 7 = M, 2 = A, 1 = S and 4 = T

5 **1425** 1 = S, 4 = T, 2 = A and 5 = R

6 **5314** 5 = R, 3 = E, 1 = S and 4 = T

7 **432** 4 = T, 3 = E and 2 = A

8 **5327** 5 = R, 3 = E, 2 = A and 7 = M

9–13 Try each of the words in the first set of brackets. Do they make sense with any words in the second and third set of brackets? Only one combination of three words makes sense.

9 **painted, picture, classroom**

10 **broke, vase, thrown away**

11 **Caterpillars, butterflies, wings**

12 **times, you, door**

13 **rose, orange, ball**

14 **bandage**

15 **behind**

16 **birthday**

17 **foolhardy**

18 **colourless**

19 **miss** 'Miss' means to overlook or lose; it is also another word for a girl or a lass.

20 **light** 'Light' means bright and well-lit; it can also mean portable or easy to carry.

21 **crib** A crib is a bed for a baby, similar to a cot or a cradle; it can also mean to copy or forge.

22 **lace** 'Lace' is related to fabric, similar to thread or string; it can also mean to fasten or tie.

23 **beam** A beam is a length of wood, similar to a timber or a pole; it can also mean a glimmer or ray.

24 **h** wish, helm

25 **k** book, knee

26 **w** grow, wish

27 **l** meal, lisp

28 **t** seat, trap

29 **spiteful** 'Mean' and 'spiteful' are synonyms in the same way as are 'hinder' and 'prevent'.

30 **below** 'Above' and 'below' are antonyms in the same way as are 'inside' and 'outside'.

31 **part** 'Clot' has been created from 'closet' by removing the fourth and fifth letters. 'Part' has been created from 'parent' in the same way.

32 **toes** 'Foot' and 'toes' go together as connected body parts in the same was as 'hand' and 'fingers'.

33 **unevenly** 'Flat' is the opposite of uneven. 'Flat' is an adjective and uneven has been changed into the adverb 'unevenly'. The opposite of 'quick' is slow, which has been changed in the same way to 'slowly'.

34 **D** MEN, DRAW

35 **L** PUMP, LAND

36 **C** LEAN, CARE

37 **R** CAVE, CART

38 **L** SEA, BRIDLE

39–43 Category A contains musical instruments (**bugle, drum, piano, guitar**)
Category B contains vegetables (**turnip, cress, onion**)
Category C contains reptiles (**adder, snake, tortoise**)

44 **PUN** puncture

45 **ARE** squares

46 **RED** watered

47 **LOW** blowing

48 **BAD** badger

49 **rear** The**re ar**e several pairs of shoes.

50 **snow** Please climb into the car**s now**.

51 **reel** The last th**ree l**etters are there.

52 **soft** The question i**s oft**en asked.

53 **lend** Soon the play wil**l end**.

54 Mum was **cooking in** the kitchen.

55 We **went** on the last **bus**.

56 You can **do** your **sums**.

57 **I** think it is **cold** today.

58 I got **all my** sums right.

59–60

B	R	E	A	D
A	■	X	■	O
R	E	A	D	S
O	■	C	■	E
N	O	T	E	S

61–62

C	O	M	E	S
H	■	O	■	P
A	P	P	L	E
I	■	E	■	N
R	E	S	E	T

63 **blue, sky** 'Green' is the colour of 'grass' in the same way as 'blue' is the colour of the 'sky'.

64 **drink, thirst** A person suffering from 'hunger' needs 'food' in the same way as a person who is suffering from 'thirst' needs 'drink'.

65 **girl, woman** A 'boy' grows up to be a 'man' in the same way as a 'girl' grows up to be a 'woman'.

66 **high, low** 'Top' is opposite to 'bottom' in the same way as 'high' is opposite to 'low'.

67 **soft, hard** 'Well' is opposite to 'ill' in the same way as 'soft' is the opposite to 'hard'.

68 **6, 3** The number subtracted decreases by 1 each time: −5, −4, −3, −2, −1.

69 **72, 24** Each number in the sequence decreases by 12.

70 **29, 38** The number added increases by 1 each time: +5, +6, +7, +8, +9.

71 **5, 38** The sequence alternately adds 7 and 6: +7, +6, +7, +6, +7.

72 **15, 13** There are two sequences which alternate. The first, third and fifth numbers follow the first sequence; the second, fourth and sixth numbers follow the second sequence. In the first sequence, the number increases by 1 each time. In the second sequence, the number increases by 2 each time.

73–76 A table is the easiest way to sort the information, like this:

	Blue	Green	Red
A	✓		
B	✓		
C		✓	✗
E		✓	
F		✓	✓

73 **green**

74 **red**

75 **1**

76 **4**

77 **BEAST**

78 **LOOPS**

79 **FRAIL**

80 **NOTES**

Paper 3 (pages 9–13)

1–5 Place the letters of the word below or above the symbols to make coding and decoding easier:

£	+	−	×	÷	@	%	/
P	U	R	C	H	A	S	E

1 **SHARES**

2 **SPRUCE**

3 @ − × ÷ / %

4 % ÷ @ − £

5 × @ % ÷

Bond Verbal Reasoning Assessment Papers 10–11+ years Book 1

6 **towels, chips** After swimming we are sometimes allowed fish and chips for supper.

7 **cream, paint** The artist dipped his brush into the blue paint on his palette.

8 **supermarket, station** The train pulled into the station and let the passengers get off.

9 **ruler, pencil** Simon sharpened his pencil over the bin.

10 **door, window** The rain fell heavily against the window pane.

11 **d** dance, date, dash, dart, done

12 **f** fare, flag, for, flash, feel

13 **w** won, wit, want, was, wedge

14 **b** blank, bloom, block, blush, bowl

15 **g** gate, gloss, grain, grind, gutter

16 **thing** The pattern is to remove 'fl' from the beginning of the first word and replace it with 'th'.

17 **shell** The pattern is to remove 't' from the beginning of the first word and replace it with 'sh'.

18 **stop** The pattern is to reverse the order of the letters.

19 **whose** The pattern is to remove 'r' from the beginning of the first word and replace it with 'wh'.

20 **mire** The pattern is to remove 'ac' from the middle of the first word and replace it with 'ir'.

21 **kidnap, abduct** Both words mean to take someone away against their will.

22 **oil, lubricate** Both words mean to add oil or grease to something.

23 **scarce, scanty** Both words mean very small in quantity.

24 **current, contemporary** Both words mean belonging to the present time.

25 **flabbergast, astound** Both words mean to astonish.

26 **coast** Shore and beach are both on the coast; 'coast' means to freewheel or glide

27 **dog** A dog is both an animal and a pet; 'dog' means to pursue or follow

28 **figure** 'Digit' and 'number' are synonyms for figure; 'figure' means the same as 'form' and 'shape'.

29 **goal** In sport, a goal, a score and a point are synonyms; 'goal' means the same as aim and target.

30 **branch** A branch, a twig and a bough are all parts of a tree; 'branch' also means a subdivision or offshoot.

31–35 Try each set of the words in the first set of brackets. Do they make sense with any words in the second and third set of brackets? Only one combination of three words makes sense.

31 **dog, barked, lead**

32 **tower, view**

33 **forests, trees, animal**

34 **computer, information**

35 **quickly, play, puddles**

36 **morning, dusk** 'Dawn' begins the 'morning' as 'dusk' begins the 'evening'.

37 **run, wings** 'Legs' are used to 'run' as 'wings' are used to 'fly'.

38 **meadow, beach** 'Grass' covers a 'meadow' as 'sand' covers a 'beach'.

39 **seven, twelve** There are seven days in a week, as there are twelve months in a year.

40 **Stop, green** 'Stop' is represented by the 'red' traffic light, as 'go' is represented by the 'green' traffic light.

41 **refuse, offer** 'Refuse' is the most opposite to 'offer' because 'refuse' means to decline whereas 'offer' means to propose.

42 **many, few** 'Many' is the most opposite to 'few' because 'many' means a large number whereas 'few' means a small number.

43 **asleep, awake** 'Asleep' is the most opposite to 'awake' because 'asleep' means unconscious whereas 'awake' means conscious.

44 **ebb, flow** 'Ebb' is the most opposite to 'flow' because 'ebb' is when the tide is moving away from the shore whereas 'flow' is when the tide is coming in towards the shore.

45 **health, ailment** 'Health' is the most opposite to 'ailment' because 'health' generally means being well whereas an 'ailment' is the same as an illness.

46 **pencil, pen** The other three words are connected to education.

47 **believe, guess** The other three words all mean to encourage.

48 **horse, trough** The other words are all animal homes.

49 **rail, road** The other words are all vehicles.

50 **nephew, father** The other words are female family names.

51 **with** withdraw, withstand, withhold, without

52 **master** masterpiece, mastermind, masterclass, masterwork

53 **after** aftercare, afternoon, after-effect, aftershock

54 **up** upstairs, upset, upright, uphill

55 **night** nightfall, nightcap, nightdress, nightlight

56–57

C		U		S	
A	N	G	L	E	S
R		L		T	
P	O	I	N	T	S
E		E		E	
T	U	R	K	E	Y

58–59

	S		C		A
E	T	C	H	E	D
	O		O		V
P	R	A	I	S	E
	M		C		R
A	S	P	E	C	T

60 **18, 29** The number added increases by 1 each time: +1, +2, +3, +4, +5, +6.

61 **96, 36** The number decreases by 12 each time.

62 **38, 30** The number subtracted decreases by 2 each time: –14, –12, –10, –8, –6, –4.

63 **13, 13** There are two sequences which alternate. The first, third, fifth and seventh numbers follow the first sequence; the second, fourth and sixth numbers follow the second sequence. In the first sequence, the number increases by 1 each time. In the second sequence, the number increases by 2 each time.

64 **4, 6** There are two sequences which alternate. The first, third, fifth and seventh numbers follow the first sequence; the second, fourth and sixth numbers follow the second sequence. In the first sequence, the number increases by 1 each time. In the second sequence, the number increases by 2 each time.

65 **2 January** (There are 31 days in December so 30 December + 3 days)

66 **23 December** (30 December – 7 days)

67 **13 January** (There are 31 days in December so 30 December + 14 days)

68–70 Arrange the words in a grid to make it easier to put them in the correct alphabetical order.

d	o	u	b	l	e
d	o	u	b	t	
d	o	u	g	h	
d	o	u	s	e	
d	o	w	n		

68 **down**

69 **double**

70 **doubt**

71 **r** tear, risk; purr, rope

72 **w** paw, work; pillow, weather

73 **b** bulb, barge; barb, bush

74 **p** wasp, pear; slip, pond.

75 **n** crown, nod; plan, noon.

76 **omen** He keeps the stamps fr**om en**velopes.

77 **scan** Mistake**s can** be easily made.

78 **wink** She gre**w ink**y-blue flowers in the garden.

79 **term** It's your turn af**ter m**ine.

80 **here** <u>He re</u>plied angrily, and ran out.

Paper 4 (pages 13–18)

1–5 Use grids as shown below to help work out the missing word.

1 REAL

	3	1	2	4				3	1	2	4	
K	E	R	B	A	S	K	S	A	J	A	R	E E L S

2 NEST

	1	2	3	4				1	2	3	4	
P	I	T	Y	P	E	A	S	B	O	N	E	S T I R

3 FOUL

2	3		4		1		2	3		4		1
T	A	I	L	T	H	A	W	S O U R	L E A F

4 BEDS

4		1		2	3		4		1		2	3	
E	N	D	S	I	C	E	D	S O B S	E D G E

5 TOOK

2	3		4		1		2	3		4		1
T	I	N	S	D	R	A	B	W O O D	K I L T

6 **PEA** speaks

7 **ONE** honey

8 **EAT** weather

9 **LAY** playing

10 **CAN** vacant

11 **therefore**

12 **outlaw**

13 **inside**

14 **handsome**

15 **capable**

16 **REVER<u>SE</u>**

17 **W<u>R</u>ING**

18 **<u>S</u>PEAK**

19 **PEA<u>C</u>E**

20 **S<u>P</u>OON**

21 **22, 37** The number added increases by 1 each time: +2, +3, +4, +5, +6, +7, +8.

22 **68, 77** The sequence alternately adds 9 and 2: +9, +2, +9, +2, +9, +2, +9.

23 **10, 15** The sequence alternately adds 3 and 1: +3, +1, +3, +1, +3, +1, +3.

24 **5, 95** The sequence alternately subtracts 1 and multiplies by 3: –1, x3, –1, x3, –1, x3, –1.

25 **75, 68** The sequence alternately subtracts 5 and adds 1: –5, +1, –5, +1, –5, +1, –5.

26 **call, whisper** The other words are all related to weather.

27 **book, programme** The other words are verbs related to seeing.

EXPANDED ANSWERS

Bond Verbal Reasoning Assessment Papers 10–11+ years Book 1

28 **face, leg** The other words are connected to colour.

29 **animal, house** The other words are verbs related to making marks with a pen.

30 **skin, jelly** The other words are fruits.

31 **MQ** Each letter in the first pair moves forward by one letter in the second pair.

32 **51** The first number in the pair is multiplied by 3 to make the second number.

33 **31** The first number in the pair is divided by 3 to make the second number.

34 **9** The second number in the pair is the square root of the first number.

35 **100** The first number in the pair is divided by 100 to make the second number.

36–40 Place the letters of the word below or above the symbol to make coding and decoding easier:

▲	❑	■	▼	○	●	◆
C	L	O	T	H	E	S

36 **SOOTHE**

37 **CLOSE**

38 **LOST**

39 **▼○■◆●**

40 **○■◆▼**

41 **fire, ice** 'Fire' is the most opposite to 'ice' because 'fire' is extremely hot whereas 'ice' is extremely cold.

42 **freeze, heat** 'Freeze' is the most opposite to 'heat' because 'freeze' is the verb for making something very cold whereas 'heat' is the verb for making something very hot.

43 **night, morning** 'Night' is the most opposite to 'morning' because 'night' is dark whereas 'morning' is light.

44 **sea, land** 'Sea' is the most opposite to 'land' because 'sea' is liquid whereas 'land' is solid.

45 **toil, rest** 'Toil' is the most opposite to 'rest' because 'toil' is a synonym for work whereas 'rest' is a synonym for leisure.

46 **faint** To faint means to blackout or feel giddy; 'faint' also means faded or unclear.

47 **blow** A gale and a blast both blow (they are types of wind); a blow is also a synonym for an upset or a calamity.

48 **charm** To charm is to attract or to please someone; a charm is also similar to a spell and relates to magic.

49 **capital** 'Capital' is a synonym for chief or main; capital also means the same as money or wealth.

50 **break** To break means to split or shatter; a break is also an interval or a holiday.

51 **ROLLING, MOSS**

52 **SEVEN, WEEK**

53 **COUNT, CHICKENS**

54 **CAPITAL, WALES**

55 **SEVEN, RAINBOW**

56 **XGJXF** To get from the word to the code, move each letter backwards five places.

57 **HFMORTSG** This is a mirror code. To get from the word to the code, number the letters of the alphabet from 1 – 13 and then 13 – 1. Look for the number of a letter, then find the letter with the same number in the other half of the alphabet. For a different way of working out mirror codes, see the answer to Paper 13 Q56.

58 **CMVF** To get from the word to the code, move each letter forwards one place.

59 **STUB** To get from the code to the word, move each letter backwards one place.

60 **DUST** To get from the code to the word, move each letter forwards two places.

61–62

S		S		N	
P	O	T	T	E	R
R		A		T	
A	S	T	U	T	E
Y		I		L	
S	I	C	K	E	N

63–64

H		K		P	
O	P	E	N	E	D
P		T		A	
I	N	T	E	N	D
N		L		U	
G	R	E	E	T	S

65 **baby**

b	a	b	y					
g	r	o	w	n	u	p		
p	e	n	s	i	o	n	e	r
s	c	h	o	o	l	g	i	r	l
s	t	u	d	e	n	t		

66 **seedling**

b	u	d					
f	l	o	w	e	r		
l	e	a	f				
s	e	e	d				
s	e	e	d	l	i	n	g

67 pushchair

b	i	c	y	c	l	e		
c	a	r						
p	r	a	m					
p	u	s	h	c	h	a	i	r
t	r	i	c	y	c	l	e	

68 letter

b	o	o	k				
l	e	t	t	e	r		
p	a	r	a	g	r	a	p	h
s	e	n	t	e	n	c	e
s	t	u	d	e	n	t	

69 quadruple

d	o	u	b	l	e		
n	o	n	e				
q	u	a	d	r	u	p	l	e
s	i	n	g	l	e		
t	r	i	p	l	e		

70 **People are not wood.** 'Some animals are kept as pets', 'People build with wood' and 'A dog is a type of animal' might well be true, but for this question you can only judge what is true based on the information given. The sentences do not say anything about pets, building, or dogs. Only 'People are not wood' can be true in this case because the sentences state that people are animals and that animals are not wood. Therefore, people are not wood.

71 **el** chisel, eldest
72 **le** handle, lead
73 **ge** change, geese
74 **al** metal, almost
75 **re** centre, read
76 **Where** is **your** big sister?
77 My **pencils** all **need** sharpening.
78 **I** made **some** scones today.
79 I **like** having my lunch **at** school.
80 I take my **dog** out each **day**.

Paper 5 (pages 18–22)

1 **foe**
2 **heir**
3 **rough**
4 **calm**
5 **middle**

6 **milk, water** A 'jug' can hold 'milk' in the same way a 'glass' can hold 'water'.
7 **come, join** 'Leave' is the opposite of 'come' in the same way as 'part' is the opposite of 'join'.
8 **scales, feathers** 'Fish' are covered in 'scales' in the same way as a 'bird' is covered in 'feathers'.
9 **you, me** 'Yours' belongs to 'you' in the same way as 'mine' belongs to 'me'.
10 **odd, normal** 'Conventional' is the opposite of 'odd' in the same way as 'abnormal' is the opposite of 'normal'.
11 **block** A block is both solid and a lump; a block can also mean an obstacle or a stop.
12 **fare** A fare can mean the same as a charge or a price; 'fare' is also another name for a meal or food.
13 **crop** To crop is to clip or trim; the noun 'crop' can also be used to mean the same as the nouns 'yield' and 'produce'.
14 **post** A post can mean the same as a column or a pole; a post is also a position or an assignment.
15 **mind** 'Mind' is associated with brain and head; to mind something is the same as to resent or dislike it.
16 **30** 7 x 6 = 42 and 30 + 12 = 42
17 **58** 9 x 9 = 81 and 11 + 58 + 12 = 81
18 **7** 14 ÷ 7 = 2 and 10 – 8 = 2
19 **47** 14 + 16 = 30 and 47 – 13 – 4 = 30
20 **5** 5 x 2 = 10 and 20 ÷ 5 + 6 = 10
21 **bad** There is no 'b' in 'dread', so this word cannot be made from its letters.
22 **tease** There is only one 'e' in 'spatter', so this word cannot be made from its letters.
23 **matter** There is only one 't' in 'cremate', so this word cannot be made from its letters.
24 **truce** There is no 'u' in 'carpenter', so this word cannot be made from its letters.
25 **stems** There is only one 's' in 'distemper', so this word cannot be made from its letters.
26 **highlight**
27 **ringlet**
28 **farewell**
29 **overboard**
30 **crossbow**
31 **tour** We tried **to ur**ge our team to win.
32 **soar** Out of breath, the last rower lent over hi**s oar**.
33 **chin** 'Whi**ch in**formation is correct?' queried the teacher.
34 **seat** When you are seated, plea**se at**tach the safety belt.
35 **scan** For old people, climbing step**s can** be difficult.
36 **sorted**

37 **haven**

38 **mined**

39 **print**

40 **bride**

41–45 Try each of the words in the first set of brackets. Do they make sense with any words in the second and third set of brackets? Only one combination of three words makes sense.

41 **car, lane, pedestrian**

42 **books, desk, lesson**

43 **Pink, colour, scarf**

44 **scene, streets**

45 **darkness, thief, window**

46 **KO** Each letter in the first pair moves forward by two letters in the second pair.

47 **DWE** The first and third letter in the first trio moves forward by one letter. The second letter in the first trio moves back by one letter.

48 **KPD** The first and second letters in the first trio move forward by two letters. The third letter in the first trio moves back by six letters.

49 **HJH** Each letter in the first trio moves forward by two letters in the second trio.

50 **LF** The first letter in the first pair moves back by two letters in the second pair. The second letter in the first pair moves forward by two letters.

51 **BEAR, BEAT**

52 **BAND, BANK**

53 **FOAM, FORM**

54 **PATS, PASS**

55 **HAND, HIND**

56–57

H	A	M
O	R	E
D	E	N

58–59

A	L	E
S	E	W
H	O	E

60 **21, 57** The number added increases by 3 each time: +3, +6, +9, +12 + 15, +18.

61 **8, 13** There are two sequences which alternate. In the first sequence, starting with 7, the number increases by 2 each time. In the second sequence, starting with 8, the number increases by 8 each time.

62 **100, 79** Each number in the sequence decreases by 7.

63 **saddle, tyre** Mia's bike had a flat tyre.

64 **east, west** As the sun set in the west, Ali watched the shadows lengthen.

65 **grass, wall** The high wall that surrounded the castle was designed to keep out the enemy.

66 **cushion, needle** I find it difficult to thread my needle in my sewing lessons.

67 **trumpet, nose** Take a tissue and blow your nose rather than sniff.

68–72 Place the letters of the word below or above the symbol to make coding and decoding easier:

@	=	=	X	@	£	@	+	÷	X
A	P	P	E	A	R	A	N	C	E

68 **CAPE**

69 **ARE**

70 **= £ X X +**

71 **+ X @ £**

72 **= £ @ + ÷ X**

73 **RULE**

74 **PLASTER**

75 **PLEASE**

76 **TRUST**

77 **OCEAN**

78 **25** 7 + 2 + 5 + 6 + 5

79 **29** 4 + 8 + 6 + 2 + 9

80 **28** 3 + 8 + 6 + 6 + 5

Paper 6 (pages 23–27)

1 **61** 10 + 20 + 12 + 6 + 8 + 5

2 **37** 12 + 6 + 4 + 10 + 5

3 **60** 8 + 12 + 6 + 4 + 20 + 10

4 **49** 10 + 8 + 6 + 4 + 4 + 5 + 12

5 **46** 20 + 12 + 6 + 8

6 **FALSE**

7 **TRAPS**

8 **TRACE**

9 **BRUSH**

10 **TABLE**

11 **PHRASE**

12 **real** They we**re al**l caught in a rainstorm.

13 **hats** He hoped t**hat s**omething would turn up.

14 **they The y**oungest toddler cried for his mother.

15 **tool** Luckily their delays were not **too l**engthy.

16 **fort** I want to run in the race **for t**he charity.

17–21 Try each of the words in the first set of brackets. Do they make sense with any words in the second and third set of brackets? Only one combination of three words makes sense.

17 **terrace, roses, pruning**

18 **book, exciting, down**

19 **drummed, car roof, school**

20 **savage, postman, letters**

21 **day, water, plants**

22 **le** purple, league

23 **ch** branch, charge

24 **sh** perish, shield

25 **ic** mosaic, icicle

26 **en** fasten, engine
27 **AE, EI** Each letter in a pair moves forward by one letter in the following pair.
28 **XM, UP** The first letter in a pair moves back by one letter in the following pair. The second letter in a pair moves forward by one letter.
29 **4X7, 6T5** The first number in a trio increases by 1 each time. The letter in the middle of a trio moves back by two letters each time. The last number in a trio decreases by 1 each time.
30 **B6, C13** The letters are in a sequence of two As, two Bs, two Cs. For the numbers, the number added increases by 1 each time: +1, +2, +3, +4, +5.
31 **11, 19** The sequence alternately adds 8 and subtracts 6: +8, -6, +8, -6, +8.
32 **rival, opponent**
33 **spine, backbone**
34 **sure, certain**
35 **bluff, pretend**
36 **brave, fearless**
37 **NEST, TENS**
38 **STEP, PEST**
39 **LEAP, PALE**
40 **WEST, STEW**
41 **LAIR, RAIL**
42 There **was** a funny smell **in** the kitchen.
43 I was three **when** my sister **was** born.
44 He **was** a very **brave** man.
45 She **sieved** the flour **into** the bowl.
46 We **will** soon **start** school.
47–51 Place the letters of the word below or above the symbol to make coding and decoding easier:

T	E	A	C	H	E	R
◗	~	○	●	▮	~	■

47 **CHEAT**
48 **ACHE**
49 **TRACE**
50 ● ■ ○ ◗ ~
51 ○ ■ ● ▮
52 **TAR** stared
53 **EAR** heard
54 **TON** tongue
55 **OAR** roared
56 **CUT** acute
57 **cupboard**
58 **crossword**
59 **foreground**
60 **deadlock**
61 **forgive**
62–66 Solve these questions by looking at the first set of three and working out how the first and last numbers have been used to arrive at the middle number. Apply this to the second set of three and see if it works. If it does, apply it to the last set.

62 **14** $9 + 2 = 11$ and $7 + 5 = 12$, so $8 + 6 = 14$
63 **3** $15 ÷ 3 = 5$ and $30 ÷ 5 = 6$, so $24 ÷ 8 = 3$
64 **15** $2 × 2 + 3 = 7$ and $2 × 6 + 7 = 19$, so $2 × 4 + 7 = 15$
65 **8** $8 + 9 + 1 = 18$ and $3 + 4 + 1 = 8$, so $6 + 1 + 1 = 8$
66 **9** $(5 × 4) ÷ 2 = 10$ and $(6 × 4) ÷ 2 = 12$, so $(9 × 2) ÷ 2 = 9$
67–71 A table is the easiest way to sort the information, like this:

	Ballroom	Judo	Fencing	Tap
Anne	✓	✓		✓
Emma	✓	✓	✓	
Lucy		✓	✓	
Caroline	✓			✓

67 **Anne**
68 **Emma**
69 **fencing**
70 **tap dancing**
71 **two**
72 **LAKE, LIKE**
73 **PILE, PILL**
74 **WOOD, WORD**
75 **COST, MOST**
76 **BLOT, BOOT**
77–80 Arrange the words in a grid to make it easier to put them in the correct alphabetical order.
77 1st is **soften**; 2nd is **lighten**; 3rd is **moisten**; 4th is **fasten**

N	E	T	F	O	S	
N	E	T	H	G	I	L
N	E	T	S	I	O	M
N	E	T	T	A	F	

78 1st is **comical**; 2nd is **musical**; 3rd is **official**; 4th is **final**

L	A	C	I	M	O	C	
L	A	C	I	S	U	M	
L	A	I	C	I	F	F	O
L	A	N	I	F			

79 1st is **oddment**; 2nd is **segment**; 3rd is **catchment**; 4th is **fitment**

T	N	E	M	D	D	O	
T	N	E	M	G	E	S	
T	N	E	M	H	C	T	A	C
T	N	E	M	A	T	I	F	

Bond Verbal Reasoning Assessment Papers 10–11+ years Book 1

EXPANDED ANSWERS

80 1st is **dancing**; 2nd is **saying**; 3rd is **flying**;
    4th is **crying**

G	N	I	C	N	A	D	
G	N	I	Y	A	S		
G	N	I	Y	L	F		
G	N	I	Y	R	C		

Paper 7 (pages 27–32)

1 **SEND, DENS**
2 **LAST, SALT**
3 **LAPSE, SEPAL**
4 **ADDER, DREAD**
5 **POST, STOP**
6 **t** rust, trend
7 **p** rose, place
8 **r** font, rice
9 **e** clan, plane
10 **b** eat, bend
11 **push, in** 'Pull' is the opposite of 'push' in the same way as 'out' is the opposite of 'in'.
12 **tilt, level** 'Lean' and 'tilt' are synonyms, as are 'flat' and 'level'.
13 **egg, seed** A 'chicken' comes from an 'egg' in the same way as 'grass' comes from a 'seed'.
14 **cherish, question** 'Adore' and 'cherish' are synonyms, as are 'doubt' and 'question'.
15 **destroy, discover** 'Ruin' and 'destroy' are synonyms, as are 'find' and 'discover'.
16–20 Start with 3844, which ends with a repeated number. Two of the given words end in a repeated letter: BALL and WALL. 3844 must be the code for either BALL or WALL, so 8 = A and 4 = L. The word WAIL also ends in L, so its code must also end in 4. Only one word doesn't end in L: BASE. Its code must be 6851. Knowing BASE = 6851 proves that B = 6, S = 5 and E = 1. The code for BALL must be 6844, so the code 3844 must be WALL, and W = 3. That leaves the code 3824, which must be for WAIL, so I = 2.

A	B	E	I	L	S	W
8	6	1	2	4	5	3

16 **6844**
17 **3824**
18 **6851**
19 **3844**
20 **LAWS**
21 **mallet** 'Hammer' and 'mallet' are both types of tools. 'Hammer' can also be used as a verb, meaning to hit repeatedly, but none of the options have this meaning.
22 **flexible** 'Elastic' and 'flexible' can both describe things that stretch and bend.
23 **ravenous** 'Hungry' and 'ravenous' both mean feeling the need for food.
24 **entire** 'Whole' and 'entire' both mean complete and undivided.
25 **cleanse** 'Wash' and 'cleanse' are both verbs meaning to make clean.
26 **holidays, birthday** 'Happy thirteenth birthday, Warren,' shouted his mother.
27 **cat, dog** The dog took her bone to her kennel and quietly ate it.
28 **soldier, Queen** The Queen waved at her subjects as she stood on the balcony at Buckingham Palace.
29 **picture, book** Jamil carefully took down a heavy reference book from the library shelf and started to read.
30 **newts, tadpoles** Our tadpoles grew legs and turned into frogs.
31 **ADD** saddle
32 **TAN** stand
33 **TAR** custard
34 **RAN** currants
35 **HER** there
36 **63, 42** Each number in the sequence decreases by 7.
37 **50, 56** The number added increases by 1 each time: +3, +4, +5, +6, +7.
38 **4, 32** Each number in the sequence is multiplied by 2.
39 **20, 10** There are two sequences which alternate. The first, third, fifth and seventh numbers follow the first sequence; the second, fourth, sixth and eighth numbers follow the second sequence. In the first sequence the number increases by 5 each time. In the second sequence the number decreases by 2 each time.
40 **100, 45** There are two sequences which alternate. The first, third, fifth and seventh numbers follow the first sequence; the second, fourth, sixth and eighth numbers follow the second sequence. In the first sequence the number increases by 10 each time. In the second sequence the number increases by 6 each time.
41 **st** almost, stance
42 **ch** trench, charge
43 **ch** broach, cheap
44 **ed** cried, edge
45 **en** ashen, enjoy
46 **7316** If the code is F = 1, L = 7, E = 3, T = 6, then LEFT = 7316.

47 **CKBMLDU** The first letter moves forward one place (P to Q) so B = C; the second letter moves back one place (I to H) so L = K; the third letter moves forward one place (L to M) so A = B; the fourth letter moves back one place (L to K) so N = M; and so on in a pattern (O to P = +1) (W to V = −1).

48 **UQHV** To get from the word to the code, move each letter forward two places.

49 **SPLASH** To get from the code to the word, move each letter forward one place. (After Z the next letter will be A as the alphabet will start again.)

50 **NWOR** To get from the word to the code, move each letter forward two places.

51 **pupil** 'Tutor' is someone who teaches so 'pupil', which means someone who learns, is the most opposite in meaning.

52 **commence** To 'end' something is to finish it so 'commence', which means to begin, is the most opposite in meaning.

53 **loosen** 'Tie' means to fix together, for instance with rope; to 'loosen' something allows it to come apart, so 'loosen' is the most opposite in meaning.

54 **descend** 'Climb' means to go up, so 'descend', which means to go down, is the most opposite in meaning.

55 **hide** 'Show means to reveal or display, so 'hide', which means to conceal, is the most opposite it meaning.

56 **paper** paperweight, paperback, paperwork, paperclip

57 **counter** counterattack, countersign, counteract, counterpart

58 **under** undertake, understand, underwear, underwater

59 **head** headgear, headlamp, headphones, headline

60 **sea** seaweed, seaside, seafront, seafood

61–62

S	P	A	R	E
O		C		A
L	A	T	E	R
I		E		L
D	A	D	D	Y

63–64

S	T	A	L	E
U		W		V
P	E	A	C	E
E		I		N
R	A	T	E	S

65–66

D	I	M	L	Y
R		E		E
O	P	E	R	A
N		T		R
E	A	S	E	S

67–71 Arrange the words in a grid to make it easier to put them in the correct alphabetical order.

F	U	R	N	A	C	E	
F	U	R	N	I	T	U	R	E
F	U	R	R	O	W		
F	U	S	E				
F	U	S	S				

67 **FURNACE**
68 **FUSS**
69 **FURROW**
70 **FUSE**
71 **FURNITURE**

72–76 Beauty was in a stable next to Halo so Beauty and Halo must be in A and B, or G and H. Trigger was next to Emily so Trigger and Emily must be in A and B, or G and H. Trigger was opposite Beauty so Trigger and Beauty must be in B and G. This means that Willow must be in stable E. Halo was not on the same side as Willow. As Willow is in stable E, Halo must be in stable H. Beauty is next to Halo so Beauty must be in stable G. Trigger was opposite Beauty so Trigger must be in stable B. Trigger was next to Emily so Emily must be in stable A.

72 **Emily**
73 **Trigger**
74 **Willow**
75 **Beauty**
76 **Halo**
77 Is **it Tuesday** or Wednesday tomorrow?)
78 Please may I **leave** the **room**?
79 Twenty-four **is** six times **four**.
80 **Silk** is as soft as cat's **fur**.

Paper 8 (pages 32–36)

1 **trap, snare** Both words mean to catch or imprison.
2 **let, allow** Both words mean to permit.
3 **too, also** Both words mean 'as well as'.
4 **bowl, dish** Both words are containers.

Bond Verbal Reasoning Assessment Papers 10–11+ years Book 1

5 **watch, survey** Both words mean to look at closely or observe.

6 Is **your** bath **too** hot?

7 I **think** it **may** snow today.

8 Did **you** leave it **at** the club?

9 I've **got** to meet **her** at 1 o'clock.

10 I put **the** book **on** the shelf.

11–15 Place the letters of the word below or above the coded word to make coding and decoding easier:

4	7	8	3	6	5	2
S	U	R	G	E	O	N

11 **4552**

12 **3526**

13 **8546**

14 **5784**

15 **NURSE**

16–20 Use grids as shown below to help work out the missing word.

16 **PEAK**

2	3	1				4		2	3	1				4
D	E	A	R		A	R	I	D		H	E	A	P		D	I	S	K

17 **MOAN**

3	1		4		2		3	1		4		2
H	A	V	E		I	C	O	N		A	M	E	N		S	O	U	R

18 **SEAL**

3	4		1			2		3	4		1			2
S	T	U	B		D	A	Z	E		A	L	E	S		T	I	M	E

19 **PORT**

2		1			3	4		2		1			3	4
P	A	N	T		B	I	K	E		L	O	O	P		C	A	R	T

20 **TURN**

3	2			1		4		3	2			1		4
L	U	C	K		C	O	L	T		R	U	S	K		T	E	E	N

21–22

	F		I		P
T	U	N	N	E	L
	T		S		A
T	I	D	I	L	Y
	L		S		E
L	E	T	T	E	R

23–24

	D		D		S
B	A	N	I	S	H
	N		R		A
S	C	R	E	A	M
	E		C		E
G	R	A	T	E	D

25–26

	S		P		A
S	P	R	A	Y	S
	R		R		T
R	E	M	O	T	E
	A		L		R
A	D	D	E	R	S

27 **te** crate, tenth

28 **el** towel, elbow

29 **in** grain, insect

30 **le** table, leaves

31 **or** motor, organ

32 **hero** He baited the hook and tested t**he ro**d.

33 **rent** It never **ent**ered my head.

34 **wash** I remember when he **was h**ead teacher.

35 **show** Few thing**s, how**ever, have shaken him.

36 **fort** He broke the school record **for t**he long jump.

37–40 Category A contains words to do with travel documents (**passport, tickets, visa**)
Category B contains words to do with land types (**rainforest, grassland, mountains**)
Category C contains words to do with weather (**tempest, gale, tornado**)
Category D contains words to do with materials (**cotton, silk, wool**)

41 **THICKEN**

42 **STABLE**

43 **REWARD**

44 **STRUNG**

45 **SOLVE**

46 **thunder** thunderstorm, thunderbolt, thundercloud, thunderclap

47 **head** headmaster, headlight, headdress, headquarters

48 **tooth** toothpaste, toothache, toothbrush, toothpick

49 **hand** handwriting, handkerchief, handshake, handcuff

50 **finger** fingernail, fingertip, fingerprint, fingermark

51 **25, 33** Each number in the sequence increases by 8.

52 59, 51 Each number in the sequence decreases by 4.

53 40, 160 Each number in the sequence is multiplied by 2.

54 11, 9 There are two sequences which alternate. The first, third, fifth and seventh numbers follow the first sequence; the second, fourth, sixth and eighth numbers follow the second sequence. In the first sequence the number increases by 3 each time. In the second sequence the number increases by 10 each time.

55 42, 9 There are two sequences which alternate. The first, third, fifth and seventh numbers follow the first sequence; the second, fourth, sixth and eighth numbers follow the second sequence. In the first sequence the number increases by 6 each time. In the second sequence the number decreases by 9 each time.

56 RAT grated

57 OUR course

58 ATE water

59 MAT match

60 OLD golden

61–65 A table is the easiest way to sort the information, like this:

	Sausages	Fish	Chips	Mashed Potatoes	Ice cream	Trifle	Coffee
A	✓		✓		✓		
B	✓			✓		✓	✓
C		✓	✓			✓	✓

61 C

62 A

63 B

64 B and **C**

65 B

66–69 Try each of the words in the first set of brackets. Do they make sense with any words in the second and third set of brackets? Only one combination of three words makes sense.

66 built, bank, river

67 constructed, wall, markets

68 film, story, sad

69 fall, lengthened, set

70 hand, finger A 'foot' has a 'toe' on it in the same way as a 'hand' has a 'finger' on it.

71 two, double 'One' is a synonym for 'single' as 'two' is for 'double'.

72 hide, animal 'Skin' covers the body of a 'man' in the same way as 'hide' covers the body of an 'animal'.

73 happy, joy 'Sad' is the adjective associated with 'sorrow' in the same way as 'happy' is the adjective associated with 'joy'.

74 pledge, promise 'Oath' is a synonym for 'vow' as 'pledge' is for 'promise'.

75 22 $6 + 7 + 3 + 1 + 5$

76 21 $8 + 3 + 3 + 7$

77 23 $6 + 7 + 3 + 1 + 6$

78 19 $7 + 3 + 1 + 8$

79 15 $4 + 1 + 2 + 3 + 5$

80 24 $6 + 7 + 1 + 2 + 3 + 5$

Paper 9 (pages 36–40)

1 loose 'Exuberant' is the opposite of 'restrained', so' fixed' is the opposite of 'loose'.

2 discipline 'Penalise' and 'discipline' are synonyms in the same way as are 'flair' and 'ability'.

3 star 'Dart' is made from the last letter and the first three letters (going backwards) of 'trapped'; so the last letter and the first three letters (going backwards) of 'rattles' spells the word 'star'.

4 fed The first letter and last two letters of 'basket' spell 'bet', so first letter and the last two letters of 'failed' spell the word 'fed'.

5 calculate 'Reckon' and 'calculate' are synonyms in the same way as are 'humid' and 'steamy'.

6 ARCH parched

7 HERE hemisphere

8 EVER several

9 LAST plaster

10 RAIN drains

11 sh brush, shove

12 ch batch, chew

13 lo halo, love

14 sh radish, shine

15 le bridle, leader

16 DOLPHINS, OCEAN

17 PYRAMIDS, RIVER

18 REPRODUCE, RATE

19 THATCHED, STRAW

20 EMERGENCY, DIAL

21 lifeless

22 setback

23 pipeline

24 outrage

25 afterwards

26 mile The pattern is to remove the 'y' from the end of the word and replace it with 'ile'.

27 stir The pattern is to begin the word with 's', followed by the first three letters in reverse order.

28 light The pattern is to use the first letter followed by the letters 'ight'.

29 spar The pattern is to use the first four letters only / remove the last two letters.

30 tire The pattern is to use the fourth, third and second letters, followed by the fifth letter.

Bond Verbal Reasoning Assessment Papers 10–11⁺ years Book 1

31 **b** ear, blink
32 **e** clan, breathe
33 **l** and, flake
34 **d** one, dwell
35 **l** spice, slide
36 I'm **sure** I've made **some** mistakes.
37 There are **some** bargains in **the** sale.
38 I **must** take my dog **for** a walk.
39 What is the **name** of that **boy**?
40 I **must** go to bed **soon**.
41 **restore** Choose the word that has most in common, making sure that it matches with all of the words outside the brackets.
42 **portion**
43 **curb**
44 **puzzling**
45 **eject**
46 **CE, EK** The first letter in the pair moves forward by one letter each time. The second letter in the pair moves forward by three letters each time.
47 **ZA, QJ** The first letter in the pair moves back by five letters then forwards by three letters, repeating the pattern. The second letter in the pair moves forward by five letters then back by three letters, repeating the pattern.
48 **KM, MI** The first letter in the pair moves forward by three letters then back by one letter, repeating the pattern. The second letter in the pair moves back by two letters each time.
49 **BC, FG** Each letter in the first pair moves forward to four letters in the following pair.
50 **UP, CL** The first letter in the pair moves forward by four letters each time. The second letter in the pair moves back by two letters each time.
51 **AD, EH** Each letter in the first pair moves forward to four letters in the following pair.
52 **27, 34** The sequence alternately adds 7 and 5: is +7, +5, +7, +5, +7, +5, +7.
53 **3, 19** The sequence alternately subtracts 2 then adds 9: –2, +9, –2, +9, –2, +9, –2.
54 **46, 82** Each number in the sequence increases by 9.
55 **9, 14** The number added increases by 1 each time: +3, +4, +5, +6, +7, +8, +9.
56 **9, 6** There are two sequences which alternate. The first, third, fifth and seventh numbers follow the first sequence; the second, fourth, sixth and eighth numbers follow the second sequence. In the first sequence the number increases by 2 each time. In the second sequence the number decreases by 1 each time.
57 **CHIORST**
58 **N** (A A A E G **N** R T T V X)

59 Arrange the words in a grid to make it easier to put them in the correct alphabetical order.

C	L	A	P		
C	L	A	S	P	
C	L	E	A	N	
C	L	I	N	G	
C	L	O	S	E	

60–61 Place the letters of the word below or above the coded word to make coding and decoding easier:

6	H	7	C	4	X
F	A	C	I	L	E

60 **FACE**
61 **CLIFF**
62–64 Place the letters of the word below or above the coded word to make coding and decoding easier:

4	X	Y	6	A	T
P	A	S	T	R	Y

62 **4XA6**
63 **6XY6T**
64 **Y6XA6**
65–66 Place the letters of the word below or above the coded word to make coding and decoding easier:

X	4	3	Y	Z
L	O	W	E	R

65 **ROWER**
66 **WOOL**
67 **Fire engines are red.** This is supported by the information, 'My car is red; so are fire engines.'
68 **Ford make cars.** This is supported by the information, 'My sister's car is a Ford.'
69 **All wasps do not have bones.** This is supported by the information: 'Wasps are insects. Insects do not have internal skeletons.'
70 **You do not need bones to fly.** This is supported by the information: 'Wasps are insects.' 'Insects do not have internal skeletons.' 'Many insects can fly.'
71–75 To complete this type of question, follow the rules of BIDMAS: complete the brackets first, then the multiplication or division and finally the addition or subtraction. In algebra, if letters or numbers are placed next to each other without a + − × or ÷ sign then multiply them.
71 **1.5** $(6 + 5 + 4) ÷ 10 = 1.5$
72 **3** $(6 × 5) ÷ 10 = 3$

73 **10** (4 x 3 ÷ 6) + 8 = 10
74 **4** (4 x 10) ÷ (2 x 5) = 4
75 **4** (2 x 10 x 8) ÷ (2 x 5 x 4) = 4
76 **music, volume** The other words are instruments.
77 **sufficient, adequate** The other words mean 'insufficient'.
78 **azure, navy** The other words are colours associated with red.
79 **outfit, material** The other words all mean 'the same'.
80 **ear, eye** The other words are all verbs related to the senses.

Paper 10 (pages 41–45)

1 **ALTER, LATER**
2 **SHRUB, BRUSH**
3 **CRATE, TRACE**
4 **STABLE, BLEATS**
5 **TOWELS, LOWEST**
6 What <u>time</u> do you <u>think</u> she will arrive?
7 I hope <u>we</u> have one of <u>her</u> special lunches.
8 Where <u>is</u> your <u>new</u> coat?
9 Do <u>you</u> think she will come <u>by</u> car?
10 I hope I <u>will</u> play <u>well</u> this afternoon.
11 **contradict, agree** 'Contradict' is most opposite to 'agree' because 'contradict' means to say the opposite of a statement is true whereas 'agree' means to say that the statement is true,
12 **guilty, innocent** 'Guilty' is the most opposite to 'innocent' because 'guilty' means having committed a crime whereas 'innocent' means not having committed a crime.
13 **reduce, increase** 'Reduce' is the most opposite to 'increase' because 'reduce' means to make smaller whereas 'increase' means to make larger.
14 **glut, insufficiency** 'Glut' is the most opposite to 'insufficiency' because 'glut' means too much of something whereas 'insufficiency' means not enough of something.
15 **divide, multiply** 'Divide' is the most opposite to 'multiply' as 'divide' is to split a number into smaller parts whereas 'multiply' is to cause a number to become larger.
16 **Sweets can be damaging to people.** This is supported by the information: 'Eating sweets can damage your teeth. Eating sweets can make you ill.' The other sentences may be true but are not supported by the information given.
17 **Some rodents make good pets.** This is supported by the information: 'Rabbits and guinea pigs are rodents. Rabbits and guinea pigs make good pets.' The other sentences may be true but are not supported by the information given.

18 **A reservoir provides water.** This is supported by the information: 'A reservoir is a lake that stores water for people to use.' The other sentences may be true but are not supported by the information given.
19 **Henry was Elizabeth's father.** This is supported by the information: 'Elizabeth I was Henry's daughter.' The other sentences may be true but are not supported by the information given.
20 **care** 'Care' and 'mind' are both verbs meaning to be bothered about.
21 **lukewarm** 'Tepid' and 'lukewarm' both mean moderately warm.
22 **treasure** 'Cherish' and 'treasure' are both verbs meaning to love and care for.
23 **bake** 'Cook' and 'bake' are both verbs to do with preparing food.
24 **stop** 'Halt' and 'stop' both mean cease or come to a standstill.
25 **96, 91** Each number in the sequence decreases by 5.
26 **72, 54** Each number in the sequence decreases by 9.
27 **17, 19** The number added decreases by 1 each time: +5, +4, +3, +2, +1.
28 **6.66, 0.666** Each number in the sequence is divided by 10.
29 **16, 18** There are two sequences which alternate. In the first sequence, starting with 6, the number increases by 6 each time. In the second sequence, starting with 16, the number increases by 4 each time.
30 **soft** The lette**rs oft**en arrived late.
31 **hats** I love the books in **t**ha**t s**eries.
32 **bean** That question cannot **be an**swered.
33 **sent** 'Thi**s ent**ails a lot of work,' moaned the pupil.
34 **rope** Mrs Brown had fou**r ope**rations on her knee.
35 **rain** rainbow, rainfall, rainproof, rainwater
36 **light** lighthouse, lightship, lighthearted, lightweight
37 **day** daydream, daybreak, daylight, daytime
38 **with** withhold, without, withdraw, within
39 **black** blackcurrant, blackmail, blackbird, blackboard
40–42 Place the letters of the word below or above the coded word to make coding and decoding easier:

H	2	G	4	Z	R
F	L	O	W	E	R

Bond Verbal Reasoning Assessment Papers 10–11+ years Book 1

40 **WELL**
41 **FLEE**
42 **RG2Z**
43–44 Place the letters of the word below or above the coded word to make coding and decoding easier:

2	4	7	3	8	X	Z
P	I	C	T	U	R	E

43 **X42Z**
44 **3X422ZX**
45–49 Arrange the words in a grid to make it easier to put them in the correct alphabetical order.

45 **forgive**

f	i	e	l	d	
f	o	r	e	i	g	n
f	o	r	f	e	i	t
f	o	r	g	i	v	e
f	u	r	r	o	w

46 **guinea**

g	r	a	c	i	o	u	s
g	u	a	r	d
g	u	i	l	d
g	u	i	n	e	a
g	y	m	n	a	s	t

47 **quintet**

q	u	e	s	t	i	o	n
q	u	i	e	t
q	u	i	l	t
q	u	i	n	t	e	t
q	u	i	t

48 **interrupt**

i	n	t	e	r	n	a	l
i	n	t	e	r	p	l	a	y
i	n	t	e	r	r	o	g	a	t	e
i	n	t	e	r	r	u	p	t
i	n	t	o

49 **penalty**

p	e	c	u	l	i	a	r
p	e	d	i	c	u	r	e
p	e	d	i	g	r	e	e
p	e	n	a	l	t	y
p	e	r	s	o	n

50 **o** halo, omen polo, office
51 **c** epic, carp; panic, coat
52 **g** thing, gnaw; plug, goat
53 **d** pond, dash; blind, deep
54 **h** clash, hark; earth, hit
55 **RAN** branch
56 **EAR** beard
57 **LAD** gladly
58 **ALL** ballot
59 **OUR** journey
60 **p** lace, pride
61 **d** anger, dread
62 **r** cease, frilly
63 **l** lance, glisten
64 **l** below, bridle
65–69 When completing this type of question, it is worth remembering that the next letter after Z will be A as the alphabet will start again.
65 **INFRTSI** To get from the word to the code, move each letter forward five places.
66 **AEVR** To get from the word to the code, move each letter forward four places.
67 **2534** If the code is B = 9, A = 3, T = 4, C = 2, H = 5 then CHAT = 2534.
68 **SMALL** To get from the code to the word, move each letter back three places.
69 **CDMKT** To get from the word to the code, move the first, third and fifth letters forward one place, and the second and fourth letters back one place: the sequence is +1, −1, +1, −1, +1.
70 **move, motion** 'Broad' is associated with 'wide' in the same way as 'move' is associated with 'motion'.
71 **overseas, abroad** 'Pant' and 'gasp' are synonyms as are 'overseas' and 'abroad'.
72 **over, under** 'Over' is the opposite of 'under' in the same way as 'win' is the opposite of 'lose'.
73 **peace, war** 'Peace' is the opposite of 'war' in the same way as 'rude' is the opposite of 'polite'.
74 **clear, lucid** 'Know' and 'understand' are synonyms as are 'clear' and lucid'.

75–76

B	U	Y	I	N	G
L		A		E	
I	N	C	H	E	D
G		H	D		
H	A	T	R	E	D
T			S	D	

77–78

	D		C		S
H	E	A	R	S	E
	C		O		A
W	I	G	W	A	M
	D		N		A
P	E	R	S	O	N

79–80

P		C		S	
R	E	A	L	L	Y
I		L		E	
V	A	L	U	E	D
E		E		V	
T	A	R	G	E	T

Paper 11 (pages 46–50)

1 **Houses are popular.** This is supported by the information, 'People like living in houses.' The other sentences may be true but are not supported by the information given.

2 **Houses need some form of heating.** This is supported by the information, 'Houses have to be heated.' The other sentences may be true but are not supported by the information given.

3 **Not all gardens are looked after.** This is supported by the information, 'Some gardens are neglected.' The other sentences may be true but are not supported by the information given.

4–5

	T		A		W
J	I	N	G	L	E
	S		R		A
A	S	S	E	S	S
	U		E		E
F	E	U	D	A	L

6–7

		B		W		Y
B	R	A	I	S	E	
		E		N		L
P	A	R	C	E	L	
		C		E		O
S	H	A	D	O	W	

8 **cool** 'Cool' means the same as fresh and unheated; it also means poised and controlled.

9 **correct** 'Correct' means the same as exact and precise; the verb 'correct' also means the same as to amend and to repair.

10 **bill** A 'bill' is a beak or nose; it is also a term associated with money, as are 'charge' and 'account'.

11 **draw** 'Draw' is a word associated with art, as are 'sketch' and 'picture'; it is also associated with gambling as 'lottery' and 'sweepstake'.

12 **claw** 'Claw' as a noun means the same as 'talon' and 'nail'; as a verb, it also means the same as to scratch and to scrape.

13 **roundabout**
14 **somehow**
15 **justice**
16 **ballroom**
17 **spokesman**
18 **pen**
19 **foal**
20 **crowd**
21 **notion**
22 **join**
23 **l** growl, lad; petal, loft
24 **a** plea, arc; banana, answer
25 **e** ease, earn; taste, elm
26 **t** might, team; toast, twin
27 **k** teak, kind; lark, kill
28 When does the next **term** **start**?
29 **I** must try to **be** neater.
30 I'd **love** a bicycle **for** my birthday.
31 Where **did** you put the **paper**?
32 It is **very** lovely **living** in the country.
33–34 To get from the word to the code, move each letter forward two places.
33 **UKZVJ**
34 **HQWTVJ**
35–37 To get from the word to the code, move each letter backward one place.
35 **EHQRS**
36 **EQNMS**
37 **AHFFDQ**

38–42 To complete this type of question, follow the rules of BIDMAS: complete the brackets first, then the multiplication or division and finally the addition or subtraction. In algebra, if letters or numbers are placed next to each other without a $+$ $-$ $\times$ or $\div$ sign then multiply them.

38 **0** $(5 \times 0) \div 2 = 0$ (Multiplying any number by 0 gives the answer 0.)

39 **0** $2 \times 10 \times 0 = 0$ (Multiplying any number by 0 gives the answer 0.)

40 **10** $3 + 5 + 0 + 2 = 10$

41 **91** $10^2 - 3^2 = 91$

42 **5** $(10 \div 5) + 3 = 5$

43 **pear** All the words are names of fruit.

44 **laugh** All the words are verbs associated with expressing laughter.

45 **enormous** All the words are adjectives meaning large.

46 **twinkle** All the words are verbs associated with sparkling.

47 **upset** All the words are verbs meaning to spill.

48 **deliver** 'Collect' means to pick up and take away; 'deliver' means to bring.

49 **result** 'Cause' means the reason why something has happened and comes before the event; 'result' is the effect something happening and comes after the event.

50 **least** 'Most' means the greatest quantity of something; 'least' means the smallest quantity of something. ('None' would imply 'nothing of something', so it is the reverse of 'some' or 'a lot'.)

51 **complete** The word 'partial' means part of something; the word 'complete' means whole.

52 **late** 'Prompt' means 'on schedule' or 'in good time'; 'late' means 'behind schedule'.

53 **trace** There is no 'e' in 'custard', so this word cannot be made from its letters.

54 **read** There is no 'r' in 'pleased', so this word cannot be made from its letters.

55 **dear** There is no 'd' in 'manager', so this word cannot be made from its letters.

56 **tart** There is only one 't' in 'depart', so this word cannot be made from its letters.

57 **hatchet** There is only one 't' and one 'h' in 'teacher', so this word cannot be made from its letters.

58 **mink** The pattern is to remove the 'k' from the beginning of the first word and replace it with 'm'.

59 **sole** The third letter becomes the first letter followed by the second, first and fourth.

60 **slowing** The root word is followed by the 'ing' suffix.

61 **rote** The fourth letter becomes the first letter and is followed by 'o', then the first and second letters.

62 **goal** The second and third letters swap places.

63 **RAIN** sp**rain**ed

64 **LIVE** de**live**red

65 **SHIN** poli**shin**g

66 **EASE** c**ease**less

67 **PENS** sus**pens**e

68 **t** rain, told

69 **a** bet, gain

70 **t** plan, tent

71 **s** mile, cosy

72 **c** rust, cold

73 **32, 16** The number divides by 2 each time.

74 **10, 27** The sequence alternately adds 7 and 5: $+7, +5, +7, +5, +7$.

75 **24, 96** The number multiplies by 2 each time.

76 **23, 30** The number added increases by 1 each time: $+3, +4, +5, +6, +7$.

77 **100, 83** The number subtracted decreases by 1 each time: $-9, -8, -7, -6, -5$.

78–80 To solve these quickly, write a shortened version of the months in alphabetical order. It is then easier to answer the questions: Apr, Aug, Dec, Feb, Jan, Jul, Jun, Mar, May, Nov, Oct, Sep

78 **September**

79 **April**

80 **August**

Paper 12 (pages 50–55)

1 **individual, different** Both words mean unlike others, unique.

2 **crime, offence** Both words mean an illegal act.

3 **value, worth** Both words mean how much importance something has, or how much money would be paid for it.

4 **obtain, acquire** Both words mean get.

5 **ordinary, normal** Both words mean usual or standard.

6–10 Use the grids as shown below to help work out the missing word.

6 **PART**

4	3		1			2		4	3		1				2	
M	I	S	T		R	A	R	E		T	R	I	P		B	E	A	N

7 **ONCE**

		1	2		4	3				1	2		4	3	
B	A	K	E		P	E	S	T		I	R	O	N		E	C	H	O

8 **SIGN**

3	2				1	4			3	2				1	4	
L	I	N	T		P	E	N	S		G	I	R	L		S	N	O	W

9 TEAM

		1	2		3	4		1	2		3	4
B	U	S	T		B	U	L	B		F	A	T	E		C	A	L	M

10 EARN

4				1	2	3		4				1	2	3
K	E	P	T		T	W	I	N		N	O	T	E		F	E	A	R

11 **CROW** crown
12 **WARM** swarmed
13 **OARS** hoarse
14 **MARK** supermarket
15 **SOUR** source
16 **e** pulse, elder; three, equal
17 **k** crank, king; break, know
18 **b** stab, boil; kerb, bee
19 **d** braid, dwell; pod, drain
20 **p** trip, pain; carp, please
21 **bead**
22 **face**
23 **deed**
24 **efface**
25 **café**
26 **keyhole**
27 **nosedive**
28 **network**
29 **loudspeaker**
30 **outlook**
31 **vein** I ha**ve in**formation for you
32 **rest** They a**re st**aying in a nearby hotel.
33 **twin** Be careful! They'll ge**t win**d of it soon.
34 **suet** You must pur**sue t**he course.
35 **sank** (The boy broke hi**s ank**le.)
36 **TRAY, TRAM**
37 **BENT, BEND**
38 **TRAP, TRIP**
39 **HOLE, HOLD**
40 **FAKE, FARE**
41–45 Try each of the words in the first set of brackets. Do they make sense with any words in the second and third set of brackets? Only once combination of three words makes sense.
41 **book, couple, travelled**
42 **cheers, world, boat**
43 **rain, snow, ground**
44 **give, cause, worker**
45 **tidied, night, bed**
46 There was a **table** with a lamp on it by the **window**.
47 He **got** up and so did **she**.
48 I **think** that is right as **far** as it goes.
49 **You** have been really helpful to **us**.
50 For the moment **nothing** was **done** at all.
51 **start, begin** 'Finish' is the opposite of 'begin' in the same way as 'complete' is the opposite of 'start'.

52 **sight, sound** A 'book' is experienced through 'sight', in the same way as a 'radio' is experienced through 'sound'.
53 **fib, honest** 'Lie' and 'fib' are synonyms in the same way as are 'truthful' and 'honest'.
54 **select, collect** 'Choose' and 'select' are synonyms in the same way as are 'gather' and 'collect'.
55 **talent, cure** 'Gift' and 'talent' are synonyms in the same way as are 'heal' and 'cure'.

56–57

A	S	P
S	I	R
S	P	Y

58–59

A	S	S
N	E	T
D	A	Y

60 **IKM, KMO** Each letter in the first trio moves forward by two letters in the following trio.
61 **CM, GQ** Each letter in the first pair moves forward by one letter in the following pair.
62 **JOX, GRV** The first letter in each trio alternates between J and G. The second letter in each trio moves forward by three letters each time. The third letter in each trio moves back by two letters each time.
63 **3A12, 8E8** For the first number in each trio, the number added increases by 1 each time: +1, +2, +3, +4, +5. The letter in the middle of the trio moves forward by two letters each time. The last number in the trio decreases by two each time.
64 **37, 31** The sequence alternately subtracts 6 and adds 1: –6, +1, –6, +1, –6.
65–67 Arrange the words in a grid to make it easier to put them in the correct alphabetical order.
65 **engine**

e	d	i	t	o	r
e	n	a	m	e	l
e	n	g	a	g	e
e	n	g	i	n	e
e	x	c	u	s	e

66 **middle**

m	i	d	d	l	e
m	i	l	l	e	t
m	i	r	r	o	r
m	o	n	k	e	y
m	o	t	i	o	n

67 shrub

h	o	u	s	e
l	e	d	g	e
l	e	v	e	l
s	h	o	v	e
s	h	r	u	b

68 ENTQ To get from the word to the code, move each letter back one place.

69 WRITE To get from the code to the word, move each letter forward one place.

70–71 To get from the code to the word, move each letter back two places.

70 NGALGA

71 FYR

72 QCR

73 Australians play a game that uses a ball. This is supported by the statement, 'Cricket and football are ball games. Australians are very good at rugby and cricket.' The sentences mentioning 'a bat' and 'football' can be ruled out as these words do not feature in the statements.

74 Cranberry sauce is sometimes served with turkey. This is supported by the statement, 'Turkey tastes good with cranberry sauce.' The sentences mentioning 'cream' and 'mince pies' can be ruled out as these words do not feature in the statements.

75 Guitars are stringed instruments. This is supported by the statement, 'Guitars are musical instruments. Guitars have strings.' This is the only option that mentions 'guitars'.

76–77 Spanish is a European language. Italians are Europeans. These are supported by the statements, 'Spanish and Italian are languages. Spain and Italy are in Europe.' There are three options that include the word 'European'; one of them also mentions 'fun' so can be ruled out.

78 flee, retreat

79 fur, coat

80 notice, message

Paper 13 (pages 55–60)

1 se amuse, seven

2 on spoon, once

3 am steam, amble

4 ve prove, verb

5 me prime, medal

6–10 To solve this, we can use logic as we read each piece of information like this:
- If the Smiths live between the Johnsons and the Bradleys they must live in Number 3 or 4.
- The Browns live opposite the Smiths so they must live in Number 3 or 4.
- The Mills live in Number 2 and as the Smiths live between the Johnsons and the Bradleys, they must live on the other side of the road to the Mills. The Smiths must live in Number 3.
- The Browns live opposite the Smiths so the Browns must live in Number 4.
- The Whites do not live opposite the Bradleys, so the Whites must live in Number 6 with the Johnsons in Number 5, and the Bradleys must live in Number 1.

6 The Bradleys live in Number 1.

7 The Smiths live in Number 3.

8 The Browns live in Number 4.

9 The Johnsons live in Number 5.

10 The Whites live in Number 6.

11 precise, stoop 'Exact' and 'precise' are synonyms in the same way as are 'crouch' and 'stoop'.

12 call, sum 'Summon' and 'call' are synonyms in the same way as are 'total' and 'sum'.

13 tale, gale 'Story' and 'tale' are synonyms in the same way as are 'storm' and 'gale'.

14 practical, rotate 'Sensible' and 'practical' are synonyms in the same way as are 'revolve' and 'rotate'.

15 own, sign 'Possess' and 'own' are synonyms in the same way as are 'omen' and 'sign'.

16 16, 30 There are two sequences which alternate. The first, third, fifth and seventh numbers follow the first sequence; the second, fourth, sixth and eighth numbers follow the second sequence. In the first sequence the number increases by 5, then 6, then 7 and so on. In the second sequence the number decreases by 1 each time.

17 11, 19 The sequence alternately adds 5 and subtracts 2: +5, −2, +5, −2, +5, −2, +5.

18 22, 29 There are two sequences which alternate. In the first sequence, starting with 7, the number added increases by 1 each time: +4, +5, +6. In the second sequence, starting with 17, each number in the sequence increases by 4.

19 4, 36 This is a sequence of squared numbers from 2^2 to 9^2.

20 13, 17 The sequence alternately adds 2 and 4: +2, +4, +2, +4, +2, +4, +2.

21 MPTF To get from the word to the code, move each letter forward one place.

22 **MJQ** To get from the word to the code, move each letter forward one place.

23–25 To move from the word to the code, move each letter forward one place.

23 **UPF**

24 **TVN**

25 **UPUBM**

26 **15** 6 + 1 + 3 + 5 = 15

27 **10** 2 + 1 + 2 + 5 = 10

28 **17** 2 + 1 + 3 + 11 = 17

29 **18** 8 + 5 + 1 + 4 = 18

30 **feel** 'Touch' 'stroke' and 'feel' are all associated with physical contact; to feel means the same as to notice and to sense.

31 **free** Complimentary and gratis both mean the same as 'free'; to free also means to untie and release.

32 **fleet** 'Fleet', 'armada' and 'flotilla' are all words meaning a group of boats or ships; 'fleet' is also a synonym for 'rapid' and 'fast'.

33 **fit** The adjective 'fit' means the same as 'well' and 'healthy'; the noun 'fit' is a synonym for 'spasm' and 'seizure'.

34 **find** The verbs 'find', 'discover' and 'reveal' are all linked to uncovering something; the noun 'find' also means the same as 'bargain' and 'windfall'.

35 **lard** The house was surrounded by a circu**lar d**rive.

36 **echo** The **cho**sen few gathered around David.

37 **arch** Edith sat in her ced**ar ch**air.

38 **seat** Wait for him plea**se at** the top of the stairs.

39 **idea** The t**ide a**ppears to be receding.

40 **pie, cake** As I cut my birthday cake, I made a wish.

41 **soft, loud** Please turn down your music, it's too loud.

42 **undo, fasten** The pilot told everyone to fasten their seatbelts and prepare for take-off.

43 **radio, television** Dad was watching the six o'clock news on the television.

44 **socks, hands** Please wash your hands before coming to the dinner table.

45 **DKTVJ** To get from the word to the code, move each letter forward two places.

46 **FRIEND** To get from the code to the word, move each letter forward two places.

47–49 To get from the word to the code, move each letter forward four places.

47 **TMGRMG**

48 **LEX**

49 **WIX**

50 **ailment**

51 **scene**

52 **leader**

53 **grate**

54 **nailed**

55–59 When completing this type of question, it is worth remembering that the next letter after Z will be A as the alphabet will start again.

55 **MIRRORS** To get from the code to the word, move the first letter back six places, the second letter back five places, the third letter back four places, the fourth letter back three places, and the fifth letter back two places. The sixth letter stays the same.

56 **HGIZRTSG** This is a mirror code. (C and X, and the two Ls and Os, are clues to this.) We can solve a mirror code with a table like this:

A	B	C	D	E	F	G	H	I	J	K	L	M
Z	Y	X	W	V	U	T	S	R	Q	P	O	N

S = H, T = G, R = I, A = Z, I = R, G = T, H = S, T = G

For a different way of working out mirror codes, the answer to Paper 4 Q57.

57 **STILE** To get from the code to the word, move each letter backwards two places.

58 **JYKPA** To get from the word to the code, move the first, third and fifth letters forward two places and move the second and fourth letters back two places: +2, −2, +2, −2, +2

59 **HEDGE** We can see that each letter has a value the same as its position in the alphabet so A = 1, B = 2, etc. 8 = H, 5 = E, 4 = D, 7 = G, 5 = E

60 **ship** shipwreck, shipmate, shipyard, shipshape

61 **blue** bluebell, blueprint, bluebottle, blueberry

62 **gold** goldfinch, goldfish, goldmine, goldsmith

63 **wheel** wheelbarrow, wheelchair, wheelwright, wheelspin

64 **green** greenfly, greenfield, greengrocer, greenhouse

65–66

		B		E		B
T	R	A	V	E	L	
		E		E		A
T	E	N	N	I	S	
		Z		T		T
B	E	A	S	T	S	

67–68

		I		S		H
U	N	I	Q	U	E	
		D		U		A
H	O	N	E	S	T	
		O		A		H
B	R	A	K	E	S	

69–70

		H		D		T
S	E	V	E	R	E	
		A		P		A
A	L	W	A	Y	S	
		T		R		E
W	H	I	T	E	R	

71 narrow, wide 'Narrow' is most opposite to 'wide' because 'narrow' means thin whereas 'wide' means broad.

72 reward, punishment 'Reward' is most opposite to 'punishment' because a 'reward' is given for good behaviour whereas a 'punishment' is given for bad behaviour.

73 blemished, flawless 'Blemished' is most opposite to 'flawless' because 'blemished' means marked or spoiled, whereas 'flawless' means unmarked or unspoiled (literally, 'without flaws').

74 free, enslave 'Free' is most opposite to 'enslave' because to 'free' means to allow someone to live and work as they want, whereas to 'enslave' means to force someone to live and work in a way they do not choose.

75–76 Arrange the words in a grid to make it easier to put them in the correct alphabetical order.

c	u	l	i	n	a	r	y
c	u	l	t	u	r	e	
c	u	p	b	o	a	r	d
c	u	r	a	b	l	e	
c	u	s	h	i	o	n	
c	u	s	t	o	m	a	r	y

77–78 Arrange the words in a grid to make it easier to put them in the correct alphabetical order.

p	r	e	c	i	o	u	s
p	r	e	c	i	p	i	c	e
p	r	e	c	i	s	e	
p	r	e	e	n			
p	r	e	t	t	y		
p	r	e	v	i	o	u	s

Precious, precipice, precise, preen, pretty, previous are in alphabetical order.

79–80 Arrange the words in a grid to make it easier to put them in the correct alphabetical order.

g	r	a	c	i	o	u	s	
g	r	a	p	e				
g	r	a	p	h				
g	r	a	p	h	i	c		
g	r	a	p	h	o	l	o	g	y
g	r	a	p	p	l	e		

Paper 14 (pages 60–64)

1 holy 'Simple' and 'easy' are synonyms in the same way as are 'divine' and 'holy'.

2 repel 'Divide' is the opposite of 'multiple' in the same way as 'charm' is the opposite of 'repel'.

3 apt 'Summit' and 'top' are synonyms in the same way as are 'suitable' and 'apt'.

4 site The last four letters of 'flames' make 'same' in the same way as the last four letters of 'whites' make 'site'.

5 DEER, DEAR

6 BENT, BEND

7 PRAM, PRAY

8 SLUM, PLUM

9 HILT, HINT

10 sullen 'Sullen', 'churlish', 'glowering' and 'sulky' all mean bad-tempered.

11 sugar 'Sugar', 'saccharine', 'molasses' and 'muscovado' are all sweeteners.

12 insect 'Fly', 'beetle' and 'moth' are all types of 'insect'.

13 father 'Father', 'uncle', 'brother' and 'son' are all male relatives.

14 horse 'Horse', 'stable', 'hay' and 'saddle' are all found together.

15 enough 'Enough', 'sufficient', 'satisfactory' and 'adequate' all mean an appropriate amount.

16 thin My dog gave bir**th in** October to five puppies.

17 tank His righ**t ank**le was broken when he fell off the wall.

18 chat Mary took a crucial cat**ch at** the start of the competition.

19 wash Kyle insisted the blue bike **was h**is.

20 thus Sukie thought the pa**th us**ually went through the churchyard.

21 germ Bruising my fin**ger m**ade me cry.

22 TV Each letter in the first pair moves back by four letters in the following pair.

23 VE The first letter in each pair moves back by one letter in the following pair. The second letter in each pair moves back by four letters in the following pair.

24 SV Each letter in the first pair moves forward by five letters in the following pair.

25 QJ The first letter in each pair moves back by three letters in the following pair. The second letter in each pair moves forward by three letters in the following pair.

26 SF The first letter in each pair moves back by one letter in the following pair. The second letter in each pair moves forward by three letters in the following pair.

27 opaque
28 light
29 hinder
30 straight
31 sole
32 entire
33 shapeless
34 parrot
35 hairstyle
36 finally
37 restore
38 STRANGE
39 PLASTER
40 SHORTEN
41 STRESSED

42–43

T	I	P
O	R	E
T	E	N

44–45

H	I	S
A	C	E
Y	E	T

46 I **tripped** **over** the step.
47 When **will** I see you **again**?
48 Granny **knitted** the jumper **for** me.
49 The weather **in** the desert is hot **and** dry.
50 The spider **caught** flies in her **web**.
51 She carried **fresh** flowers in **her** basket.
52 **12** $(6 \times 6) \div 2 = 18$ and $(7 \times 8) \div 2 = 28$, so $(5 \times 12) \div 2 = 30$
53 **3** $13 - 9 - 2 = 2$ and $7 - 4 - 2 = 1$, so $11 - 6 - 2 = 3$
54 **18** $(8 \times 4) \div 2 = 16$ and $(5 \times 20) \div 2 = 50$, so $(6 \times 6) \div 2 = 18$
55 **21** $4 \times 5 \times 3 = 60$ and $2 \times 4 \times 3 = 24$, so $7 \times 1 \times 3 = 21$
56 **25** $13 + 11 - 6 = 18$ and $8 + 12 - 6 = 14$, so $17 + 14 - 6 = 25$

57–61 Use grids as shown below to help work out the missing word.

57 PRAM

2	4		1	3			2	4		1	3	
B	R	I	M		F	O	O	T		T	R	A	M		P	E	A	R

58 DESK

	2		3	4	1			2		3	4	1
T	Y	P	E		S	T	O	P		C	A	R	E		S	K	I	D

59 TINT

	3	4	1		2			3	4	1		2
M	I	L	K		S	L	U	M		B	E	N	T		T	H	I	S

60 REEF

3	2	1	4			3	2	1	4	
G	O	O	D		M	O	O	D		B	E	E	R		F	L	A	N

61 TACT

3	2		1			4	3	2		1		4
B	U	S	T		B	A	R	S		C	A	R	T		J	U	S	T

62–65 Three of the words, BORE, CARE and ROBE, end in E. Two of the codes end in 1 so E = 1. One code does not end in 1 – 6347 – so this must be the code for CRAB. Therefore C = 6, R = 3, A = 4 and B = 7. CARE = 6431. The two other words are BORE and ROBE; the code 3271 must be ROBE, so O = 2.

A	B	C	E	O	R
4	7	6	1	2	3

3271 = ROBE
6347 = CRAB
6431 = CARE
7231 = BORE

62 REAR
63 BEAR
64 7231
65 73461
66 re spare, remind
67 el parcel, elder
68 dy remedy, dyed
69 on spoon, once
70 le table, lemon
71 11 $12 \times 2 = 24 = 8 + 5 + 11$
72 41 $9 \times 3 = 27 = 41 - 14$
73 3 $9 \times 2 = 18 = 36 \div 3 + 6$
74 69 $23 + 14 = 37 = 69 - 24 - 8$
75 16 $72 \div 8 = 9 = 16 - 7$

Bond Verbal Reasoning Assessment Papers 10–11+ years Book 1

76–77 When completing this type of question, it is worth remembering that the next letter after Z will be A as the alphabet will start again.

76 ZMYNC To get from the word to the code, move the first, third and fifth letters back two places, and move the second and fourth letters forward one place: the sequence is –2, +1, –2, +1, –2

77 ERROR To get from the code to the word, move the first, third and fifth letters forward two places and move the second and fourth letters back one place: the sequence is +2, –1, +2, –1, +2 (

78 N (A E L **N** P R T)
79 K (C E I **K** Q R U)
80 O (A F L **O** R V U)

Look at the first group of three words. The word in the middle has been made from the other two words. Complete the second group of three words in the same way, making a new word in the middle of the group.

Example   PAIN INTO TOOK   ALSO <u>SOON</u> ONLY

16 DEAR READ ARID   HEAP _____ DISK

17 HAVE ACHE ICON   AMEN _____ SOUR

18 STUB BEST DAZE   ALES _____ TIME

19 PANT TAKE BIKE   LOOP _____ CART

20 LUCK CULT COLT   RUSK _____ TEEN

Fill in the crosswords so that all the given words are included. You have been given one letter as a clue in each crossword.

21–22

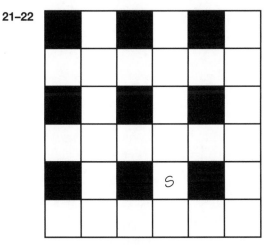

tunnel, letter, player, futile,
insist, tidily

23–24

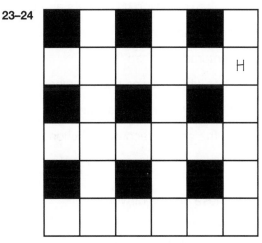

dancer, shamed, grated, direct,
banish, scream

25–26

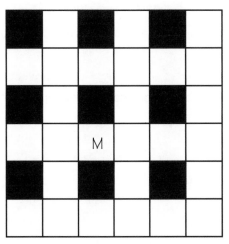

sprays, remote, asters, parole,
spread, adders

33

Find the two letters which will end the first word and start the second word.

B 10

> **Example**   rea (c̲ h̲) air

27 cra   (__ __)   nth

28 tow   (__ __)   bow

29 gra   (__ __)   sect

30 tab   (__ __)   aves

31 mot   (__ __)   gan

5

Find the four-letter word hidden at the end of one word and the beginning of the next word. The order of the letters may not be changed.

B 21

> **Example**   The children had bats and balls.   _sand_

32 He baited the hook and tested the rod.   _____

33 It never entered my head.   _____

34 I remember when he was head teacher.   _____

35 Few things, however, have shaken him.   _____

36 He broke the school record for the long jump.   _____

5

37–40   Look at these groups of words.

B 1

A	B	C	D
travel documents	land types	weather	materials

Choose the correct group for each of the words below. Write in the letter.

rainforest __   passport __   tempest __   cotton __   gale __   tickets __

visa __   grassland __   silk __   mountains __   tornado __   wool __

4

Rearrange the letters in capitals to make another word. The new word has something to do with the first two words.

B 16

> **Example**   spot   soil   SAINT   _STAIN_

41 widen   enlarge   KITCHEN   _____

42 firm   secure   BLEATS   _____

43 prize   honour   DRAWER   _____

44 threaded   hung   GRUNTS   _____

45 answer   decode   LOVES   _____

5

Find a word that can be put in front of each of the following words to make a new, compound word.

B 11

Example   cast   fall   word   pour   _down_

46 storm   bolt   cloud   clap   _____

47 master   light   dress   quarters   _____

48 paste   ache   brush   pick   _____

49 writing   kerchief   shake   cuff   _____

50 nail   tip   print   mark   _____

Give the two missing numbers in the following sequences.

B 23

Example   2   4   6   8   _10_   _12_

51 17   __   __   41   49   57

52 __   55   __   47   43   39

53 5   10   20   __   80   __

54 3   __   6   21   __   31   12   41

55 24   36   30   27   36   18   __   __

Find the three-letter word which can be added to the letters in capitals to make a new word. The new word will complete the sentence sensibly.

B 22

Example   The cat sprang onto the MO.   _USE_

56 The cook GED the cheese.   _____

57 He wanted to play golf on the new CSE.   _____

58 She bathed the cut with cold WR.   _____

59 The team was beaten in the CH.   _____

60 Her hair was a lovely GEN colour.   _____

A, B and C went out for a meal. A and B had sausages and C had fish.
A and C had chips and B had mashed potatoes.
A had ice cream.
B and C had trifle.
B and C had coffee.

B 25

61 Who had fish, chips and trifle?   _____

62 Who had sausages, chips and ice cream?   _____

63 Who had sausages, mashed potato and trifle?   _____

64 Who had trifle and coffee?   _____

65 Who had coffee but no chips?   _____

Complete the following sentences by selecting the most sensible word from each group of words given in the brackets. Underline the words selected.

Example The (children, books, foxes) carried the (houses, books, steps) home from the (greengrocer, library, factory).

66 It was the Romans who (sailed, built, paid) a city on the north (bank, bunk, back) of the (river, county, London).

67 The Romans (bought, constructed, enjoyed) a huge (wall, ladder, slope) around the town and they also built (discos, studios, markets).

68 At the end of the (road, film, cinema) the girls left crying because the (story, seats, cars) had been so (boring, sad, hard).

69 As night began to (fall, land, sea), the shadows (watched, lengthened, tightened) and the sun (sat, set, rose).

 4

Choose two words, one from each set of brackets, to complete the sentences in the best way.

Example Smile is to happiness as (drink, tear, shout) is to (whisper, laugh, sorrow).

70 Foot is to toe as (elbow, leg, hand) is to (finger, thumb, glove).

71 One is to single as (four, two, set) is to (add, double, twins).

72 Skin is to man as (tail, claw, hide) is to (animal, cat, baby).

73 Sad is to sorrow as (please, happy, hate) is to (pleading, joy, outing).

74 Oath is to vow as (pledge, memo, rule) is to (argue, promise, follow).

 5

If A = 1, C = 2, E = 3, F = 4, D = 5, T = 6, R = 7, P = 8, find the sum of these words when the letters are added together.

75 tread = ___   76 peer = ___   77 treat = ___

78 reap = ___   79 faced = ___   80 traced = ___

 6

Now go to the Progress Chart to record your score!   Total ◯ 80

Paper 9

Look at the pair of words on the left. Underline the one word in the brackets that goes with the word outside the brackets in the same way as the first two words go together.

Example good, better   bad, (naughty, worst, <u>worse</u>, nasty)

1 exuberant, restrained   fixed, (fastened, loose, secure, happy)

2 flair, ability   penalise, (discipline, goal, wrong, offside)

3 trapped, dart   rattles, (start, lest, rate, star)

4 basket, bet   failed, (led, fed, ail, aid)

5 humid, steamy   reckon, (former, further, calculate, notice)

 5

Find the four-letter word which can be added to the letters in capitals to make a new word. The new word will complete the sentence sensibly.

B 22

Example   They enjoyed the BCAST.   <u>ROAD</u>

6   I am so hot and thirsty I feel PED.   _____

7   Brazil is in the southern HEMISP   _____

8   They chose SAL of the items because one was not enough.   _____

9   The PER has come off the cut on my finger.   _____

10   The blocked DS overflowed.   _____

5

Find two letters which will end the first word and start the second word.

B 10

Example   rea (<u>c</u> <u>h</u>) air

11   bru   (__ __)   ove

12   cat   (__ __)   ew

13   ha   (__ __)   ve

14   radi   (__ __)   ine

15   brid   (__ __)   ader

5

Rearrange the muddled words in capital letters in the following sentences so that they make sense.

B 16

Example   There are sixty SNODCES <u>seconds</u> in a UTMINE <u>minute</u>.

16   OISPDLHN _____ are aquatic mammals that live in the NEACO _____.

17   You will find the SMDIYRAP _____ in Egypt by the VERIR _____ Nile.

18   Rabbits RRPCDOEUE _____ at an alarming TEAR _____.

19   HHCTATDE _____ roofs are made of reeds or TARWS _____.

20   In an MGRNYEECE _____ LAID _____ 999.

5

Underline two words, one from each group, that go together to form a new word. The word in the first group always comes first.

B 8

Example   (hard, <u>green</u>, for)   (light, <u>house</u>, sure)

21   (birth, life, cradle),   (less, more, much)

22   (pick, slow, set),   (end, back, forward)

23   (smoke, pipe, match),   (wire, water, line)

24   (out, inside, walk),   (warm, rage, temper)

25   (before, after, soon),   (theatre, bed, wards)

5

Change the first word of the third pair in the same way as the other pairs to give a new word.

Example　　bind, hind　　bare, hare　　but, <u>hut</u>

26　why, while　　　sty, stile　　　my, _____

27　pole, slop　　　nape, span　　　rite, _____

28　fatter, fight　　matter, might　　latter, _____

29　mother, moth　　tinsel, tins　　spares, _____

30　flame, male　　blast, salt　　　write, _____

Move one letter from the first word and add it to the second word to make two new words.

Example　　hunt　　sip　　<u>hut</u>　　<u>snip</u>

31　bear　　link　　_____　　_____

32　clean　　breath　　_____　　_____

33　land　　fake　　_____　　_____

34　done　　well　　_____　　_____

35　splice　　side　　_____　　_____

Find and underline the two words which need to change places for each sentence to make sense.

Example　　She went to <u>letter</u> the <u>write</u>.

36　I'm some I've made sure mistakes.

37　There are the bargains in some sale.

38　I for take my dog must a walk.

39　What is the boy of that name?

40　I soon go to bed must.

Underline the word in the brackets which goes best with the words given outside the brackets.

Example　　word, paragraph, sentence　　(pen, cap, <u>letter</u>, top, stop)

41　mend, renew, repair　　　　　　(break, damage, restore, injure, fixture)

42　part, section, piece　　　　　　(whole, portion, none, full, potion)

43　rein, check, guide　　　　　　　(curb, bridle, saddle, loose, encourage)

44　misleading, confusing, baffling　　(revolved, puzzling, complain, reflex, turning)

45　dislodge, displace, shift　　　　(rehouse, eject, disorder, dismay, distant)

Give the two missing pairs of letters in the following sequences. The alphabet has been written out to help you.

B 23

A B C D E F G H I J K L M N O P Q R S T U V W X Y Z

	Example	CQ	DP	EQ	FP	*GQ*	*HP*
46	BB	___	DH	___	FN	GQ	
47	___	UF	XC	SH	VE	___	
48	FS	IQ	HO	___	JK	___	
49	___	___	JK	NO	RS	VW	
50	QR	___	YN	___	GJ	KH	
51	OR	SV	WZ	___	___	IL	

6

Give the two missing numbers in the following sequences.

B 23

	Example	2	4	6	8	*10*	*12*		
52	3	10	15	22	___	___		39	46
53	5	___	12	10	___	17		26	24
54	___	55	64	73	___	91		100	109
55	2	5	___	___	20	27		35	44
56	3	12	5	11	7	9		___	___

5

57 Write the letters of the word OSTRICH in the order in which they appear in the dictionary.

_____

B 20

58 If the letters in the following word are arranged in alphabetical order, which letter comes in the middle?

EXTRAVAGANT

_____

59 Write the following words in alphabetical order.

CLEAN   CLAP   CLASP   CLING   CLOSE

_____ _____ _____ _____ _____

3

If the code for FACILE is 6H7C4X, what do the following codes stand for?

B 24

60 6H7X _____   61 74C66 _____

If the code for PASTRY is 4XY6AT, what are the codes for the following words?

62 PART _____   63 TASTY _____   64 START _____

If the code for LOWER is X43YZ, what do the following codes stand for?

65 Z43YZ _____   66 344X _____

7

39

Read the first two statements and then underline two of the options below that must be true.

67–68 'My car is red; so are fire engines. My sister's car is a Ford. Ford make vans.'

All Ford cars are red.   I like Ford cars.

My car is a Ford.   Ford make fire engines.

I have a fire engine.   Ford make cars.

My sister's car is red.   Fire engines have a siren.

Fire engines are red.   My sister is a firefighter.

Read the first three statements and then underline two of the options below that must be true.

69–70 'Wasps are insects. Insects do not have internal skeletons. Many insects can fly.'

Wasps have a nasty sting.   All insects are wasps.

Wasps have yellow and black stripes.   Insects have 3 parts to their bodies.

All wasps do not have bones.   Wasps like rotting fruit.

You do not need bones to fly.   All insects fly.

Angry wasps should be avoided.

If a = 10, b = 8, c = 6, d = 5, e = 4, f = 3 find the value of the following.

71 $(c + d + e) \div a =$ ___

72 $cd \div a =$ ___

73 $(ef \div c) + b =$ ___

74 $\dfrac{4a}{2d} =$ ___

75 $\dfrac{2ab}{2de} =$ ___

Underline the two words which are the odd ones out in the following groups of words.

Example	black	<u>king</u>	purple	green	<u>house</u>
76 guitar	music	piano	drums	volume
77 scarce	infrequent	sufficient	adequate	rare
78 crimson	azure	navy	scarlet	ruby
79 alike	uniform	outfit	similar	material
80 smell	speak	ear	sneeze	eye

Paper 10

B 7

Underline the two words which are made from the same letters.

Example   TAP   PET   <u>TEA</u>   POT   <u>EAT</u>

1 ALTER	ALTAR	TALLER	LATER	BLEAT	RATTER
2 CRUSH	SHRUB	CRASH	BLURB	BRUISE	BRUSH
3 BRAKE	STRIKE	CRATE	TRACE	TRACK	STACK
4 STRANGE	STAGE	LABEL	STABLE	BLEATS	BLOATER
5 TOWELS	LOWEST	SLOWER	WORST	LAWYER	FLOWER

5

Find and underline the two words which need to change places for each sentence to make sense.

B 17

Example   She went to <u>letter</u> the <u>write</u>.

6 What think do you time she will arrive?

7 I hope her have one of we special lunches.

8 Where new your is coat?

9 Do by think she will come you car?

10 I hope I well play will this afternoon.

5

Underline the pair of words most opposite in meaning.

B 9

Example   cup, mug   coffee, milk   <u>hot, cold</u>

11 contradict, agree	tired, weary	cold, shivering
12 disease, sickness	hint, suggestion	guilty, innocent
13 reduce, increase	bad, evil	require, need
14 submit, yield	glut, insufficiency	means, resources
15 milk, water	angry, cross	divide, multiply

5

Read the first two statements and then underline one of the four options below that must be true.

B 25

16 'Eating sweets can damage your teeth. Eating sweets can make you ill.'

People who are ill have bad teeth.

People with bad teeth have eaten too many sweets.

Sweets can be damaging to people.

People who are ill have been eating too many sweets.

Read the first two statements and then underline one of the four options below that must be true.

17 'Rabbits and guinea pigs are rodents. Rabbits and guinea pigs make good pets.'

    All rodents live in cages.

    All pets are rodents.

    Some rodents make good pets.

    Rabbits eat carrots.

Read the first two statements and then underline one of the five options below that must be true.

18 'A reservoir is a lake that stores water for people to use. Lake Windermere is in Cumbria.'

    Cumbria is a reservoir.

    Lake Windermere is a reservoir.

    People use Lake Windermere.

    A reservoir provides water.

    People drink the water from Lake Windermere.

Read the first two statements and then underline one of the four options below that must be true.

19 'Henry VIII had six wives. Elizabeth I was Henry's daughter.'

    Henry's family name was Tudor.

    Henry was Elizabeth's father.

    Elizabeth was a good queen.

    Henry and Elizabeth ruled for many years.

4

Underline the word in the brackets closest in meaning to the word in capitals.

B 5

	Example	UNHAPPY	(unkind	death	laughter	<u>sad</u>	friendly)
20	MIND	(stay		wait	care	fuss	rest)
21	TEPID	(hot		soapy	lukewarm	soft	cool)
22	CHERISH	(hate		treasure	annoy	ignore	reject)
23	COOK	(ingredients	recipe		oven	heat	bake)
24	HALT	(rest		pause	unsure	stop	hesitate)

5

Give the two missing numbers in the following sequences.

B 23

	Example	2	4	6	8	<u>10</u>	<u>12</u>		
25	111	106	101	___	___	86			
26	81	___	63	___	45	36			
27	5	10	14	___	___	20			
28	666	66.6	___	___	0.0666				
29	6	___	12	20	___	24	24	28	

5

Find the four-letter word hidden at the end of one word and the beginning of the next word. The order of the letters may not be changed.

B 21

Example   The children had bats and balls.   _sand_

30 The letters often arrived late.   _____

31 I love the books in that series.   _____

32 That question cannot be answered.   _____

33 'This entails a lot of work', moaned the pupil.   _____

34 Mrs Brown had four operations on her knee.   _____

5

Find a word that can be put in front of each of the following words to make new, compound words.

B 11

Example   cast   fall   ward   pour   _down_

35 bow   fall   proof   water   _____

36 house   ship   hearted   weight   _____

37 dream   break   light   time   _____

38 hold   out   draw   in   _____

39 currant   mail   bird   board   _____

5

If the code for FLOWER is H2G4ZR, what do the following codes stand for?

B 24

40 4Z22 _____   41 H2ZZ _____

Write the code for the following word.

42 ROLE _____

If the code for PICTURE is 24738XZ, what are the codes for the following words?

43 RIPE _____   44 TRIPPER _____

5

If these words were placed in alphabetical order, which word would come 4th?

B 20

45 forgive   field   forfeit   foreign   furrow   _____

46 gymnast   guild   gracious   guard   guinea   _____

47 quintet   quilt   quiet   question   quit   _____

48 interrupt   into   internal   interplay   interrogate   _____

49 pedicure   person   peculiar   penalty   pedigree   _____

5

Find the letter which will complete both pairs of words, ending the first word and starting the second. The same letter must be used for both pairs of words.

Example   mea (t̲) able   fi (t̲) ub

50 hal (_) men   pol (_) ffice

51 epi (_) arp   pani (_) oat

52 thin (_) naw   plu (_) oat

53 pon (_) ash   blin (_) eep

54 clas (_) ark   eart (_) it

5

Find the three-letter word which can be added to the letters in capitals to make a new word. The new word will complete the sentence sensibly.

Example   The cat sprang onto the MO.   USE

55 There was a BCH of the bank nearby.   _____

56 He looked different with a BD.   _____

57 I will GLY do it for you.   _____

58 Put your vote in the BOT box.   _____

59 The JNEY was long and tiring.   _____

5

Move one letter from the first word and add it to the second word to make two new words.

Example   hunt   sip   hut   snip

60 place   ride   _____   _____

61 danger   read   _____   _____

62 crease   filly   _____   _____

63 glance   listen   _____   _____

64 bellow   bride   _____   _____

5

Solve the problem by working out the letter code. The alphabet has been written out to help you.

A B C D E F G H I J K L M N O P Q R S T U V W X Y Z

Example   If the code for SECOND is written as UGEQPF, what is the code for THIRD?   VJKTF

65 If the code for JEWEL is OJBJQ, what is the code for DIAMOND?   _____

66 If the code for ALARM is EPEVQ, what is the code for WARN?   _____

67 If the code for BATCH is 93425, what is the code for CHAT?   _____

68 If the code for TINY is WLQB, what does VPDOO mean?   _____

69 If the code for RINSE is SHORF, what is the code for BELLS?   _____

5

Choose two words, one from each set of brackets, to complete the sentences in the best way.

Example Smile is to happiness as (drink, <u>tear</u>, shout) is to (whispers, laugh, <u>sorrow</u>).

70 Broad is to breadth as (month, move, more) is to (motion, use, modern).

71 Pant is to gasp as (up, overseas, side) is to (down, abroad, little).

72 Win is to lose as (over, soft, gentle) is to (on, under, between).

73 Rude is to polite as (peace, hate, fight) is to (height, war, enemy).

74 Know is to understand as (clear, clean, clever) is to (dirty, land, lucid).

5

Fill in the crosswords so that all the given words are included. You have been given one letter as a clue in each crossword.

75–76

buying, hatred, blight, needed, yachts, inched

77–78

hearse, person, seaman, decide, wigwam, crowns

79–80

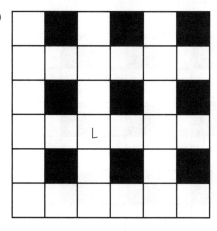

valued, caller, target, privet, sleeve, really

6

Now go to the Progress Chart to record your score! Total **80**

45

Paper 11

Read the first two statements and then underline one of the four options below that must be true.

1 'People like living in houses. Houses are usually made of brick.'

    Some people live in flats.

    Houses are popular.

    Houses have gardens.

    All houses are built of brick.

Read the first two statements and then underline one of the four options below that must be true.

2 'Houses have to be heated. Most people have central heating.'

    People don't have coal fires now.

    Houses need some form of heating.

    Everyone has central heating.

    Central heating is better than other forms of heating.

Read the first two statements and then underline one of the four options below that must be true.

3 'Most houses have a garden. Some gardens are neglected.'

    Not all gardens are looked after.

    Some people are keen gardeners.

    Some people are too busy to garden.

    All gardens have flowers.

Fill in the crosswords so that all the given words are included. You have been given one letter as a clue in each crossword.

4–5

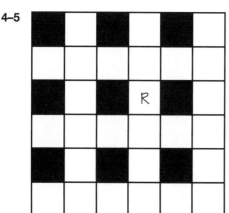

jingle, agreed, feudal, weasel,
assess, tissue

6–7

breach, yellow, braise, winced,
parcel, shadow

46

Underline the one word in the brackets which will go equally well with both the pairs of words outside the brackets.

> **Example**   rush, attack   cost, fee   (price, hasten, strike, <u>charge</u>, money)

8   fresh, unheated   poised, controlled   (cold, cool, windy, damp, calm)

9   exact, precise   amend, repair   (tool, dart, correct, fault, fix)

10   beak, nose   charge, account   (bill, bird, man, fee, receipt)

11   sketch, picture   lottery, sweepstake   (paint, pull, draw, ticket, pool)

12   talon, nail   scratch, scrape   (clay, scissors, claw, beak, point)

Underline two words, one from each group, that go together to form a new word. The word in the first group always comes first.

> **Example**   (hand, <u>green</u>, for)   (light, <u>house</u>, sure)

13   (circus, round, stalls)   (under, about, place)

14   (some, most, many)   (when, the, how)

15   (bat, just, catch)   (fast, drop, ice)

16   (string, ball, loop)   (net, room, team)

17   (spin, pedal, spokes)   (air, ring, man)

Find a word that is similar in meaning to the word in capital letters and that rhymes with the second word.

> **Example**   CABLE   tyre   *wire*

18   COOP   when   _____

19   PONY   bowl   _____

20   MASS   loud   _____

21   IDEA   ocean   _____

22   UNITE   coin   _____

Find the letter which will complete both pairs of words, ending the first word and starting the second. The same letter must be used for both pairs of words.

> **Example**   mea (<u>t</u>) able   fi (<u>t</u>) ub

23   grow (_) ad   peta (_) oft

24   ple (_) rc   banan (_) nswer

25   eas (_) arn   tast (_) lm

26   migh (_) eam   toas (_) win

27   tea (_) ind   lar (_) ill

Find and underline the two words which need to change places for each sentence to make sense.

Example   She went to <u>letter</u> the <u>write</u>.

28 When does the next start term?

29 Be must try to I neater.

30 I'd for a bicycle love my birthday.

31 Where paper you put the did?

32 It is living lovely very in the country.

A B C D E F G H I J K L M N O P Q R S T U V W X Y Z

If the code for SECOND is UGEQPF, what are the codes for the following words?

33 SIXTH   ————————

34 FOURTH   ————————

If the code for STOUT is RSNTS, what are the codes for the following words?

35 FIRST   ————————

36 FRONT   ————————

37 BIGGER   ————————

If $a = 5$, $b = 2$, $c = 0$, $d = 10$, $e = 3$, find the value of the following calculations.

38 $\dfrac{ac}{b} =$ ___

39 $bdc =$ ___

40 $e + a + c + b =$ ___

41 $d^2 - e^2 =$ ___

42 $(d \div a) + e =$ ___

Underline the word in brackets which goes best with the words given outside the brackets.

Example   word, paragraph, sentence   (pen, cap, <u>letter</u>, top, stop).

43 apple, pineapple, melon   (carrot, cauliflower, pear, cabbage)

44 giggle, chortle, chuckle   (sigh, month, happy, moan, laugh)

45 huge, vast, immense   (big, enormous, normal, high, long)

46 glitter, shine, sparkle   (twinkle, star, tinsel, lights, glare)

47 empty, spill, tip   (stir, break, sorry, upset, fill)

Underline one word in the brackets which is most opposite in meaning to the word in capitals.

Example   WIDE   (broad   vague   long   <u>narrow</u>   motorway)

48 COLLECT   (papers   letters   deliver   box   gather)

49 CAUSE   (result   aid   win   lose   reason)

50 MOST   (none   lot   least   multitude   greatest)

51 PARTIAL   (potion   portion   slice   complete   share)

52 PROMPT   (urge   late   quick   immediate   force)

5

Underline the one word which **cannot be made** from the letters of the word in capital letters.

Example   STATIONERY   stone   tyres   ration   <u>nation</u>   noisy

53 CUSTARD   rust   crust   trace   curd   dust

54 PLEASED   plea   dale   deep   read   seed

55 MANAGER   dear   game   mean   near   ream

56 DEPART   part   trade   tart   trap   dear

57 TEACHER   rate   each   hatchet   chart   hear

5

Change the first word of the third pair in the same way as the other pairs to give a new word.

Example   bind, hind   bare, hare   but, <u>hut</u>

58 kind, mind   kiss, miss   kink, _____

59 page, gape   last, salt   lose, _____

60 cleanest, slowest   clean, slow   cleaning, _____

61 rent, tore   veal, love   tear, _____

62 blot, bolt   from, form   gaol, _____

5

Find the four-letter word which can be added to the letters in capitals to make a new word. The new word will complete the sentence sensibly.

Example   They enjoyed the BCAST.   <u>ROAD</u>

63 Carys jumped off the wall and SPED her ankle.   _____

64 The postman DERED the letters.   _____

65 He enjoys POLIG his shoes.   _____

66 Their CLESS chatter was annoying.   _____

67 The film was scary and full of SUSE.   _____

5

Move one letter from the first word and add it to the second word to make two new words.

B 13

	Example	hunt	sip	<u>hut</u>	<u>snip</u>
68	train	old	_____	_____	
69	beat	gin	_____	_____	
70	plant	ten	_____	_____	
71	miles	coy	_____	_____	
72	crust	old	_____	_____	

5

Give the two missing numbers in the following sequences.

B 23

	Example	2	4	6	8	<u>10</u>	<u>12</u>
73	128	64	___	___	8	4	
74	3	___	15	22	___	34	
75	3	6	12	___	48	___	
76	5	8	12	17	___	___	
77	___	91	___	76	70	65	

5

If the months were put in alphabetical order, which would be:

B 20

78 the last month? _____

79 the first month? _____

80 the month after April? _____

3

Now go to the Progress Chart to record your score!   Total   80

Paper 12

Underline the two words, one from each group, which are closest in meaning.

B 3

Example   (race, shop, <u>start</u>)   (finish, <u>begin</u>, end)

1 (individual, looks, charm)   (different, similar, personal)

2 (law, emergency, crime)   (disorder, policeman, offence)

3 (burden, flaw, value)   (thick, worth, loyal)

4 (counter, obtain, expensive)   (acquire, buy, shop)

5 (ordinary, plain, fancy)   (vague, safe, normal)

5

Look at the first group of three words. The word in the middle has been made from the other two words. Complete the second group of three words in the same way, making a new word in the middle of the group.

B 18

Example   PAIN INTO TOOK   ALSO <u>SOON</u> ONLY

6 MIST TRIM RARE   TRIP ——— BEAN

7 BAKE KEEP PEST   IRON ——— ECHO

8 LINT PILE PENS   GIRL ——— SNOW

9 BUST STUB BULB   FATE ——— CALM

10 KEPT WINK TWIN   NOTE ——— FEAR

5

Find the four-letter word which can be added to the letters in capitals to make a new word. The new word will complete the sentence sensibly.

B 22

Example   They enjoyed the BCAST.   <u>ROAD</u>

11 The king wore his magnificent N on special occasions.   ———

12 The bees SED from the hive.   ———

13 Her voice is quite HE from cheering the team on.   ———

14 She went to the SUPERET for the weekly shop.   ———

15 The CE of the river was up in the hills.   ———

5

Find the letter which will complete both pairs of words, ending the first word and starting the second. The same letter must be used for both pairs of words.

B 10

Example   mea (<u>t</u>) able   fi (<u>t</u>) ub

16 puls (——) lder   thre (——) qual

17 cran (——) ing   brea (——) now

18 sta (——) oil   ker (——) ee

19 brai (——) well   po (——) rain

20 tri (——) ain   car (——) lease

5

Which word in each group contains only the first six letters of the alphabet?

B 18

Example   defeat farce abide <u>deaf</u> dice

21 arrow   bead   beach   creed   bread

22 adder   badge   each   face   dance

23 dread   cadge   deed   ache   decks

24 feeds   daft   fall   coffee   efface

25 card   café   feeble   buff   dabble

5

Underline two words, one from each group, that go together to form a new word. The word in the first group always comes first.

Example (hand, green, for) (light, house, sure)

26 (hammer, axe, key) (wood, tool, hole)

27 (month, nose, frown) (dive, walk, run)

28 (fish, catch, net) (duty, work, offer)

29 (soft, loud, noise) (rumble, quiet, speaker)

30 (out, under, place) (see, look, watch)

5

Find the four-letter word hidden at the end of one word and the beginning of the next word. The order of the letters may not be changed.

Example The children had bats and balls. *sand*

31 I have information for you. _____

32 They are staying in a nearby hotel. _____

33 Be careful! They'll get wind of it soon. _____

34 You must pursue the course. _____

35 The boy broke his ankle. _____

5

Change the first word into the last word, by changing one letter at a time and making two new, different words in the middle.

Example CASE *CASH* *WASH* WISH

36 FRAY _____ _____ TEAM

37 DENT _____ _____ BAND

38 TRAY _____ _____ GRIP

39 MOLE _____ _____ HELD

40 LAKE _____ _____ FARM

5

Complete the following sentences by selecting the most sensible word from each group of words given in the brackets. Underline the words selected.

Example The (children, books, foxes) carried the (houses, books, steps) home from the (greengrocer, library, factory).

41 The (look, book, watch) was about a (duet, jingle, couple) who (cried, travelled, ice-skated) around Australia.

42 Three (cheers, claps, drinks) for the yachtswoman who circumnavigated the (sea, world, sitting room) in her (slippers, rocket, boat).

43 The weatherman said that we can expect (rain, weather, nothing) today with (snow, sand, sea travel) on high (tea, ground, beach).

44 'Please (give, take, support) generously to the (effect, cause, because)', begged the charity (shop, worker, card).

45 Tessa (painted, dirtied, tidied) her bedroom each (hour, night, week) before she went to (lunch, France, bed).

5

B 17

Find and underline the two words which need to change places for each sentence to make sense.

Example She went to <u>letter</u> the <u>write</u>.

46 There was a window with a lamp on it by the table.

47 He she up and so did got.

48 I far that is right as think as it goes.

49 Us have been really helpful to you.

50 For the moment done was nothing at all.

5

B 15

Complete the following sentences in the best way by choosing one word from each set of brackets.

Example Tall is to (tree, <u>short</u>, colour) as narrow is to (thin, white, <u>wide</u>).

51 Complete is to (short, start, satisfied) as finish is to (attempt, begin, win).

52 Book is to (sight, page, cover) as radio is to (sound, music, news).

53 Lie is to (sit, fib, bed) as truthful is to (anger, honest, stand).

54 Choose is to (study, select, drop) as gather is to (collect, scatter, break).

55 Gift is to (talent, borrow, holiday) as heal is to (sell, want, cure).

5

B 19

Fill in the crosswords so that all the given words are included. You have been given one letter as a clue in each crossword.

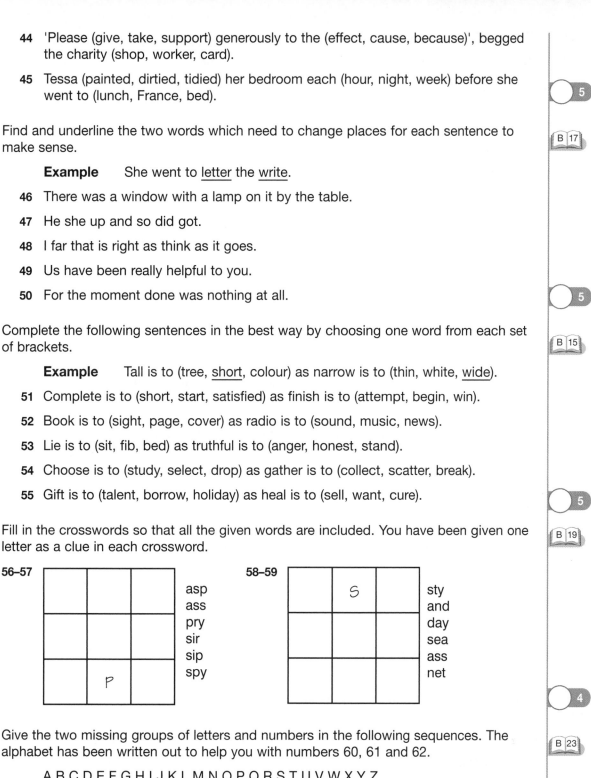

56–57

asp
ass
pry
sir
sip
spy

P

58–59

S

sty
and
day
sea
ass
net

4

B 23

Give the two missing groups of letters and numbers in the following sequences. The alphabet has been written out to help you with numbers 60, 61 and 62.

A B C D E F G H I J K L M N O P Q R S T U V W X Y Z

Example CQ DP EQ FP <u>GQ</u> <u>HP</u>

60 ACE CEG EGI GIK _____ _____

61 BL _____ DN EO FP _____

62	JCF	GFD	JIB	GLZ	_____	_____
63	2Y14	_____	5C10	_____	12G6	17I4
64	47	41	42	36	_____	_____

If these words were placed in alphabetical order:

65 engine   excuse   engage   enamel   editor

Which word would be fourth? _____

66 motion   mirror   middle   millet   monkey

Which word would be first? _____

67 ledge   shove   house   level   shrub

Which word would be last? _____

A B C D E F G H I J K L M N O P Q R S T U V W X Y Z

If the code for PRIME is OQHLD, what is the code for the following word?

68 FOUR _____

If the code for KETTLE is JDSSKD, what does the following code stand for?

69 VQHSD _____

If the code for SECOND is QCAMLB, what are the codes for the following words?

70 PICNIC _____

71 HAT _____

72 SET _____

Read the first two statements and then underline one of the four options below that must be true.

73 'Cricket and football are ball games. Australians are very good at rugby and cricket.'

Australians play a game that uses a ball.

Cricket is played with a bat.

Australians are very good at football.

Rugby is played with a bat.

Read the first two statements and then underline one of the four options below that must be true.

74 'Turkey and mince pies are often eaten at Christmas. Turkey tastes good with cranberry sauce.'

Mince pies taste good with cranberry sauce.

Turkey is best with cream.

Cranberry sauce is sometimes served with turkey.

Cream is only eaten at Christmas.

Read the first two statements and then underline one of the four options below that must be true.

75 'Guitars are musical instruments. Guitars have strings.'

All musical instruments have strings.

All musical instruments need electricity.

Guitars are stringed instruments.

Strings are musical instruments.

Read the first two statements and then underline two of the four options below that must be true.

76–77 'Spanish and Italian are languages. Spain and Italy are in Europe.'

Spanish is a European language.

European languages are fun to learn.

Italians are Europeans.

People who speak Spanish also often speak Italian.

5

Underline the two words in each line which are most similar in type or meaning.

B 5

| **Example** | dear | pleasant | poor | extravagant | expensive |

78	flee	paint	exercise	retreat	drive
79	shoe	comb	eye	fur	coat
80	song	book	notice	law	message

3

Now go to the Progress Chart to record your score! Total 80

Paper 13

Find the two letters which will end the first word and start the second word.

B 10

Example rea (c h) air

1 amu (— —) ven

2 spo (— —) ce

3 ste (— —) ble

4 pro (— —) rb

5 pri (— —) dal

5

There are six houses in a street. They are arranged like this:

1	3	5

2	4	6

The Smiths live between the Johnsons and the Bradleys.

The Browns live opposite the Smiths.

The Mills live in Number 2.

The Whites do not live opposite the Bradleys.

Who lives in each house?

Number 1 _____   Number 4 _____

Number 2 _Mills_   Number 5 _____

Number 3 _____   Number 6 _____

5

Complete the following sentences in the best way by choosing one word from each set of brackets.

Example   Tall is to (tree, <u>short</u>, colour) as narrow is to (thin, white, <u>wide</u>).

11 Exact is to (precise, please, like) as crouch is to (stoop, slap, crow).

12 Summon is to (avoid, super, call) as total is to (submit, consider, sum).

13 Story is to (bedtime, recital, tale) as storm is to (wet, cold, gale).

14 Sensible is to (practical, clever, brainy) as revolve is to (circus, rotate, fair).

15 Possess is to (present, own, prize) as omen is to (ornament, gift, sign).

5

Give the two missing numbers in the following sequences.

Example   2   4   6   8   <u>10</u>   <u>12</u>

16	7	12	11	17	___	23	22	___
17	8	13	___	16	14	___	17	22
18	7	17	11	21	16	25	___	___
19	___	9	16	25	___	49	64	81
20	5	7	11	___	___	19	23	25

5

A B C D E F G H I J K L M N O P Q R S T U V W X Y Z

B 24

If the code for HOLD is IPME, what is the code for the following word?

21 LOSE _____

If the code for PENCIL is QFODJM, what is the code for the following word?

22 LIP _____

If the code for FOOT is GPPU, what are the codes for the following words?

23 TOE _____

24 SUM _____

25 TOTAL _____

5

If A = 1, B = 2, C = 3 and so on, what is the sum of the following words if the letters are added together?

B 26

26 FACE = _____

27 BABE = _____

28 BACK = _____

29 HEAD = _____

4

Underline the one word in the brackets which will go equally well with both the pairs of words outside the brackets.

B 5

Example rush, attack   cost, fee   (price, hasten, strike, <u>charge</u>, money)

30 touch, stroke   notice, sense   (feel, like, feign, hold, announce)

31 complimentary, gratis   untie, release   (charge, free, cost, nothing, loose)

32 armada, flotilla   rapid, fast   (fleet, short-lived, army, sea, float)

33 well, healthy   spasm, seizure   (fit, ill, old, shaky, unwell)

34 discover, reveal   bargain, windfall   (finish, find, luck, key, deal)

5

Find the four-letter word hidden at the end of one word and the beginning of the next word. The order of the letters may not be changed.

B 21

Example The children had bats and balls.   <u>sand</u>

35 The house was surrounded by a circular drive.   _____

36 The chosen few gathered around David.   _____

37 Edith sat in her cedar chair.   _____

38 Wait for him please at the top of the stairs.   _____

39 The tide appears to be receding.   _____

5

Change one word so that the sentence makes sense. Underline the word you are taking out and write your new word on the line.

Example I waited in line to buy a <u>book</u> to see the film. *ticket*

40 As I cut my birthday pie, I made a wish. _____

41 Please turn down your music, it's too soft. _____

42 The pilot told everyone to undo their seatbelts and prepare for take-off. _____

43 Dad was watching the six o'clock news on the radio. _____

44 Please wash your socks before coming to the dinner table. _____

5

A B C D E F G H I J K L M N O P Q R S T U V W X Y Z

B 24

If the code for EQUAL is GSWCN, what is the code for the following word?

45 BIRTH _____

If the code for MUDDLE is KSBBIC, what does the following code stand for?

46 DPGCLB _____

If the code for HUNDRED is LYRHVIH, what are the codes for the following words?

47 PICNIC _____   48 HAT _____   49 SET _____

5

Underline the one word in each group which **can be made** from the letters of the word in capital letters.

B 7

Example CHAMPION   camping   notch   peach   cramp   <u>chimp</u>

50 PARLIAMENT   temper   plural   lemon   ailment   trait

51 DESCENDANT   scene   desert   second   tender   tandem

52 DELIVERANCE   render   cream   verge   driver   leader

53 TRIANGLE   elegant   grate   ranger   tingles   letter

54 DEALING   ailing   gleaning   ideas   nailed   landing

5

Solve the problem by working out the letter code. The alphabet has been written out to help you.

B 24

A B C D E F G H I J K L M N O P Q R S T U V W X Y Z

Example If the code for SECOND is UGEQPF, what is the code for THIRD? *VJKTF*

55 If the code for CLIMATE is IQMPCUE, what does SNVUQSS mean? _____

56 If the code for CROOKED is XILLPVW, what is the code for STRAIGHT? _____

57 If the code for BLISTER is DNKUVGT, what does UVKNG mean? _____

58 If the code for SMOOTH is UKQMVF, what is the code for HAIRY? _____

59 If the code for FACE is 6135, what does 85475 mean? _____

5

Find a word that can be put in front of each of the following words to make new, compound words.

	Example	cost	fall	ward	pour	_down_
60	wreck	mate	yard	shape	
61	bell	print	bottle	berry	
62	finch	fish	mine	smith	
63	barrow	chair	wright	spin	
64	fly	field	grocer	house	

Fill in the crosswords so that all the given words are included. You have been given one letter as a clue in each crossword.

65–66

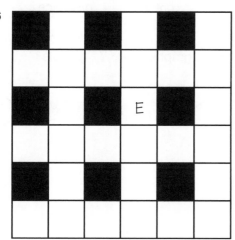

blasts, beasts, breeze, events, tennis, travel

67–68

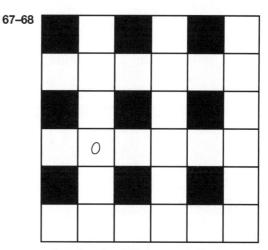

heaths, brakes, squeak, indoor, honest, unique

69–70

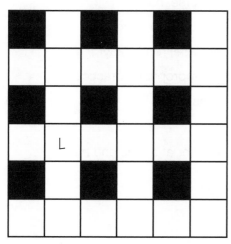

always, teaser, whiter, health, severe, depart

6

Underline the two words, one from each group, which are the most opposite in meaning.

Example (down, <u>early</u>, wake) (<u>late</u>, stop, sunrise)

71 (tall, narrow, jumping) (slender, wide, bean)

72 (annoy, discomfort, reward) (punishment, painless, distress)

73 (outcome, perfect, blemished) (effect, flawless, flat)

74 (job, expensive, free) (work, dear, enslave)

Write the words in each line in alphabetical order.

75–76 cushion customary culinary culture cupboard curable

—————— —————— —————— —————— —————— ——————

77–78 precise precious pretty previous preen precipice

—————— —————— —————— —————— —————— ——————

79–80 graphic graph gracious grape graphology grapple

—————— —————— —————— —————— —————— ——————

Now go to the Progress Chart to record your score! **Total** 80

Paper 14

Look at the pair of words on the left. Underline the one word in the brackets that goes with the word outside the brackets in the same way as the first two words go together.

Example good, better bad, (naughty, worst, <u>worse</u>, nasty)

1 simple, easy divine, (separate, holy, devilish, hard)

2 divide, multiply charm, (pendant, necklace, repel, stay)

3 summit, top suitable, (apt, peak, inappropriate, practical)

4 flames, same whites, (wits, stew, west, site)

Change the first word into the last word by changing one letter at a time and making two new, different words in the middle.

Example CASE <u>CASH</u> <u>WASH</u> WISH

5 DEEP ———— ———— YEAR

6 DENT ———— ———— BAND

7	PRIM	_____ _____	PLAY
8	SLIM	_____ _____	PLUS
9	HALT	_____ _____	MINT

5

Underline the word in the brackets which goes best with the words given outside the brackets.

B 1

Example   word, paragraph, sentence   (pen, cap, <u>letter</u>, top, stop)

10 churlish, glowering, sulky   (cheerful, sullen, sultan, glowing, silky)

11 saccharine, molasses, muscovado   (flour, sweet, sugar, hive, cheese)

12 fly, beetle, moth   (worm, kangaroo, mushroom, insect, deer)

13 uncle, brother, son   (grandmother, niece, aunt, cousin, father)

14 stable, hay, saddle   (dog, girl, horse, gerbil, bull)

15 sufficient, satisfactory, adequate (enough, lots, less, more, horde)

6

Find the four-letter word hidden at the end of one word and the beginning of the next word. The order of the letters may not be changed.

B 21

Example   The children had bats and balls.   <u>sand</u>

16 My dog gave birth in October to five puppies.   _____

17 His right ankle was broken when he fell off the wall.   _____

18 Mary took a crucial catch at the start of the competition.   _____

19 Kyle insisted the blue bike was his.   _____

20 Sukie thought the path usually went through the churchyard. _____

21 Bruising my finger made me cry.   _____

6

Fill in the missing letters. The alphabet has been written out to help you.

B 23

A B C D E F G H I J K L M N O P Q R S T U V W X Y Z

Example   AB is to CD as PQ is to <u>RS</u>.

22 NP is to JL as XZ is to _____.

23 HT is to GP as WI is to _____.

24 DG is to IL as NQ is to _____.

25 ZA is to WD as TG is to _____.

26 VW is to UZ as TC is to _____.

5

Find a word that is opposite in meaning to the word in capital letters and that rhymes with the second word.

Example   SHARP   front   <u>blunt</u>

27   TRANSPARENT   drake   _____

28   DARKNESS   quite   _____

29   HELP   cinder   _____

30   CURVED   hate   _____

31   MANY   bowl   _____

32   PARTIAL   liar   _____

Underline two words, one from each group, that go together to form a new word. The word in the first group always comes first.

Example   (hand, <u>green</u>, for)   (light, sure, <u>house</u>)

33   (shape, kind, for)   (more, less, care)

34   (per, par, pore)   (rat, rent, rot)

35   (some, shop, hair)   (style, form, who)

36   (find, fin, den)   (dolly, ally, all)

37   (rest, time, for)   (late, to, ore)

Rearrange the letters in capitals to make another word. The new word has something to do with the first two words or phrases.

Example   spot   soil   SAINT   <u>STAIN</u>

38   bizarre   unusual   GARNETS   _____

39   cover thickly   daub   STAPLER   _____

40   contract   compress   THRONES   _____

41   pressurised   strained   DESSERTS   _____

Fill in the crosswords so that all the given words are included. You have been given one letter as a clue.

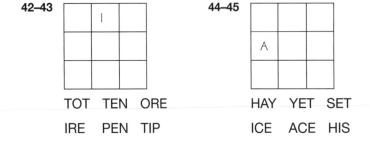

42–43

TOT   TEN   ORE
IRE   PEN   TIP

44–45

HAY   YET   SET
ICE   ACE   HIS

Find and underline the two words which need to change places for each sentence to make sense.

Example   She went to <u>letter</u> the <u>write</u>.

46 I over tripped the step.

47 When again I see you will?

48 Granny for the jumper knitted me.

49 The weather and the desert is hot in dry.

50 The spider web flies in her caught.

51 She carried her flowers in fresh basket.

6

Find the missing number by using the two numbers outside the brackets in the same way as the other sets of numbers.

Example   2 [8] 4   3 [18] 6   5 [25] 5

52 6 [6] 18   7 [8] 28   5 [___] 30

53 13 [2] 9   7 [1] 4   11 [___] 6

54 8 [16] 4   5 [50] 20   6 [___] 6

55 4 [60] 5   2 [24] 4   7 [___] 1

56 13 [18] 11   8 [14] 12   17 [___] 14

5

Look at the first group of three words. The word in the middle has been made from the other two words. Complete the second group of three words in the same way, making a new word in the middle of the group.

Example   PAIN   INTO   TOOK   ALSO   <u>SOON</u> ONLY

57 BRIM   FROM   FOOT   TRAM   _____ PEAR

58 TYPE   PEST   STOP   CARE   _____ SKID

59 MILK   SULK   SLUM   BENT   _____ THIS

60 GOOD   DOOM   MOOD   BEER   _____ FLAN

61 BUST   TUBS   BARS   CART   _____ JUST

5

Match the right code to each of the words below. One of them has been missed out. Then answer the questions below.

BORE   CARE   CRAB   ROBE

3271   6347   6431

62 Decode, using the same code, 3143. _____

63 What is 7143?   _____

64 What is the missing code? _____

65 What is BRACE in this code? _____

Find the two letters which will end the first word and start the second word.

Example rea (<u>c</u> <u>h</u>) air

66 spa (__ __) mind

67 parc (__ __) der

68 reme (__ __) ed

69 spo (__ __) ce

70 tab (__ __) mon

Find the missing number that makes the sum make sense.

Example $6 \times 2 = \underline{4} + 8$

71 $12 \times 2 = \underline{\ \ } + 8 + 5$

72 $\underline{\ \ } - 14 = 9 \times 3$

73 $9 \times 2 = 36 \div \underline{\ \ } + 6$

74 $23 + 14 = \underline{\ \ } - 24 - 8$

75 $72 \div 8 = \underline{\ \ } - 7$

76 If the code for FAULT is D B S M R, What is the code for BLAME? _____

77 Using the same code, decode C S P P P. _____

If the letters in the following words are arranged in alphabetical order, which letter comes in the middle?

78 PLANTER _____

79 QUICKER _____

80 FLAVOUR _____

Now go to the Progress Chart to record your score! Total 80

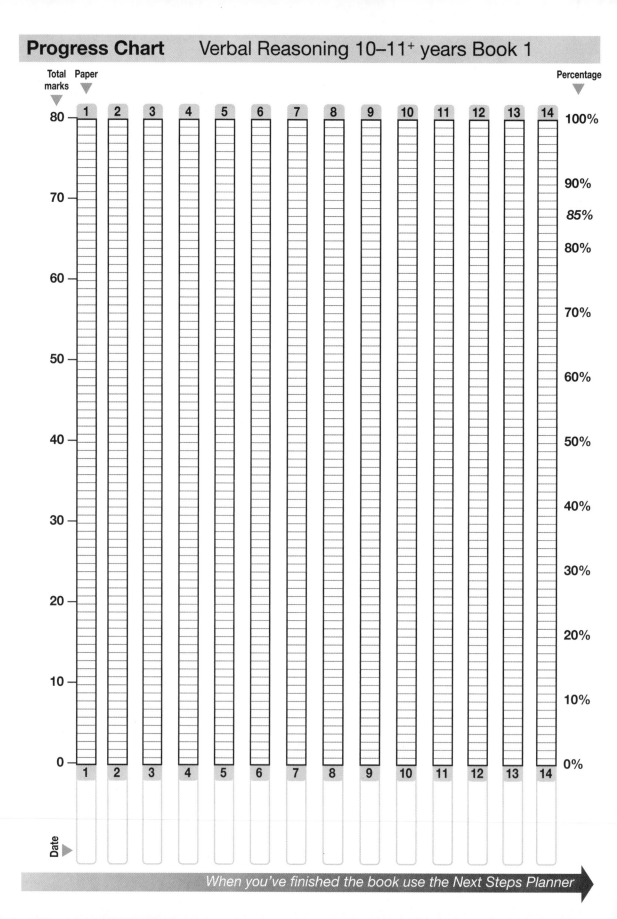